Ronald Reagan's 1984

James Cooper · R. J. Richardson · Bailey Schwab

Ronald Reagan's 1984

Politics, Policy, and Culture

James Cooper
School of Humanities
York St John University
York, UK

R. J. Richardson
School of Humanities
York St John University
York, UK

Bailey Schwab
School of Humanities
York St John University
York, UK

ISBN 978-3-031-53676-2   ISBN 978-3-031-53677-9   (eBook)
https://doi.org/10.1007/978-3-031-53677-9

© The Editor(s) (if applicable) and The Author(s), under exclusive license to Springer
Nature Switzerland AG 2024

This work is subject to copyright. All rights are solely and exclusively licensed by the
Publisher, whether the whole or part of the material is concerned, specifically the rights
of translation, reprinting, reuse of illustrations, recitation, broadcasting, reproduction on
microfilms or in any other physical way, and transmission or information storage and
retrieval, electronic adaptation, computer software, or by similar or dissimilar methodology
now known or hereafter developed.
The use of general descriptive names, registered names, trademarks, service marks, etc.
in this publication does not imply, even in the absence of a specific statement, that such
names are exempt from the relevant protective laws and regulations and therefore free for
general use.
The publisher, the authors, and the editors are safe to assume that the advice and information in this book are believed to be true and accurate at the date of publication. Neither
the publisher nor the authors or the editors give a warranty, expressed or implied, with
respect to the material contained herein or for any errors or omissions that may have been
made. The publisher remains neutral with regard to jurisdictional claims in published maps
and institutional affiliations.

Cover illustration: © Melisa Hasan

This Palgrave Macmillan imprint is published by the registered company Springer Nature
Switzerland AG
The registered company address is: Gewerbestrasse 11, 6330 Cham, Switzerland

Paper in this product is recyclable.

Acknowledgements

This project simply would not have been possible without the support of the 'students as researchers' scheme at York St John University. This ensured that Rebecca and Bailey brought their expertise and made this work infinitely stronger than it otherwise would have been—thank you both. My thanks therefore must go also to Emma Sunley at our university's research office for having confidence in our plans in the first place. Likewise, I appreciate the help of Lucy Kidwell and Saranya Siva at Palgrave, and, of course, the insightful comments from our anonymous peer reviewers. Work on this project coincided with Danielle and I welcoming our third son—and a baby brother for Macaulay and Fox. This work is therefore dedicated to Wilder River Cooper.

Jim Cooper

My thanks, as ever, to Professor Robert Edgar, who's steered my academic work for nearly a decade, against all odds. Thanks to Dr. Jim Cooper for entertaining my thoughts about popular culture and to the York St. John team for establishing the Students as Researcher programme. Thanks also to Robert Vessey, for debating history, politics and philosophy with me in turbulent times. And thanks to Messrs. Gurnham, O'Farrell & Priestley of King Edward's, who made sure I knew exactly where we'd been before I considered where we're headed.

And of course, to the wondrous Mark, Evie, Georgia, Fee and Liz.

R. J. Richardson

vi ACKNOWLEDGEMENTS

First and foremost, I would like to thank Dr Jim Cooper for allowing me to take part in this project. Thanks to Jim, this will be my first major co-authored publication. I also would like to thank York St. John's research office for giving the green light to make this project happen.

Bailey Schwab

CONTENTS

Introduction	1
1984	21
Looking Ahead to Re-election	21
Campaigning Abroad	37
Election Campaign Ads	43
The General Election	57
Conclusion	91
Select Bibliography	103
Index	105

About the Authors

James Cooper is an Associate Professor of History and American Studies at York St John University. He was previously a Senior Lecturer in History at Oxford Brookes University, UK, and he was the 20th Fulbright-Robertson Visiting Professor of British History at Westminster College, Missouri, United States and has also been a Visiting Fellow at the Norwegian Nobel Institute. His previous publications include: *A Diplomatic Meeting: Reagan, Thatcher, and the Art of Summitry* (Lexington: University Press of Kentucky, 2022); *The Politics of Diplomacy: U.S. Presidents and the Northern Ireland Conflict, 1967–1998* (Edinburgh: Edinburgh University Press, 2017); and *Margaret Thatcher and Ronald Reagan: A Very Political Special Relationship* (Basingstoke: Palgrave, 2012).

R. J. Richardson is a Postgraduate Researcher at York St John University. Her Practice as Research PhD thesis considers the concept of authenticity in long form drama, through the creation and analysis of a complete first season of a noir television show set in New York City in 1945. Her research interests lie at the intersection of historical events and fictional narrative, the nature of authenticity for a writer, the effect of music on the writing process, language as music and character psychology. She has taught on the Writing Genres B.A. Creative Writing module at York St John. Her previous work has explored performance, dramaturgy and devising and she was a Head of Drama at a secondary school for five years. Her play, *Decoy*, was performed at the York Literature Festival (2015)

x   ABOUT THE AUTHORS

and her stories, *Jatai* and *Blind Corner*, were published in York St John's *New Writing* (2015). Alongside her series, she is currently developing a crossover novel and two collections of short stories.

Bailey Schwab is a Ph.D. Student at York St. John University undertaking a thesis in U.S. presidential history between 1981 and 2009. His thesis looks at the concept of the foreign policy doctrine and how they are utilised in the critique of presidential leadership in foreign policy. He also works for a British policy think tank as a foreign policy researcher and is a member of the Ronald Reagan Foundation's scholarly roundtables for which he attends conferences with leading academics and American officials to discuss new scholarship regarding the Reagan presidency. He has had book reviews and articles published in journals such as *Intelligence and National Security* and *E-International Relations*.

Introduction

Abstract This introductory chapter contextualises Ronald Reagan's 1984. It does so by outlining the key claims of the entire work, namely that 1984 is key to understanding the lasting impact of Reagan on American politics and policy-making, Reaganism on American culture, and how the Reagan years influenced the institution of the U.S. presidency. The historiography of Reagan and his era is also explored. Similarly, the broader scholarship related to the 1980s popular culture is introduced. The chapter uses polling data to consider how Reagan was viewed in the 1980s and by Americans in more recent years.

Keywords Reagan · Reaganism · Polling · U.S. presidency · 1984 presidential election

The top three U.S. presidents among scholars in regular surveys are cited as being George Washington, Abraham Lincoln, and Franklin D. Roosevelt.[1] The issue of how to be considered among that elite pantheon—or even how they compare among their predecessors—is one that inevitably occupies the mind of any incumbent of the Oval Office and leading members of their administration. President Barack Obama was no exception. HW Brands recalled that at a meeting held at the White House between prominent American historians and Obama, the

© The Author(s), under exclusive license to Springer Nature 1
Switzerland AG 2024
J. Cooper et al., *Ronald Reagan's 1984*,
https://doi.org/10.1007/978-3-031-53677-9_1

historians were asked about how U.S. presidents can be remembered as being 'great'. Brands noted that Washington, Lincoln and Roosevelt had each been president at times of crises. As the nation's inaugural president, Washington had to ensure that the American experiment would endure in the aftermath of independence and establishment of the Republic. Lincoln kept the nation together by winning the civil war. Roosevelt had to guide the United States out of the Great Depression and lead the world in a war against fascism. Therefore, unless Obama desired an epoch defining crisis, being a 'great' president was not possible. However, Brands explained that it would be better to aim for the 'second tier' of U.S. presidential legacies, meaning those who win re-election and influence the national discourse in terms of their own political philosophy. By winning a second term and influencing and shaping national discourse and politics in his chosen direction, Obama fulfilled Brands' criteria.[2] Ronald Reagan certainly met this threshold too. Yet the fortieth president's legacy was secured not just by his landslide re-election in 1984. Key aspects of the Reagan administration's agenda—and, in turn, its impact on American politics and culture—correlated around the year of 1984.

George Orwell's dystopian novel, *1984*, was written as a warning against totalitarianism.[3] While Reagan's opponents cite that he ushered in economic inequalities and rampant and unregulated capitalism, proponents of Reagan point to his record of fierce rhetoric against communism, particularly during his first term, and demand that the West stand up to forces of totalitarianism led by what he called the 'evil empire' of the Soviet Union. Either way, Orwell was perhaps correct to look to the 1980s as being a significant decade. Indeed, 1983–1984 was arguably the highpoint of the Cold War. Tensions were so high that even the president's joke—recorded on a live microphone—in August 1984, that he had 'signed legislation, outlawing Russia forever' and that bombing was to commence 'in five minutes', briefly put the Soviet military on red alert.[4] Walter Mondale (former U.S. Vice President and the Democrats' 1984 presidential nominee) was not amused, suggesting that Reagan should be 'very careful about the words he chooses'.[5] The president was criticised further afield too. For instance, *Le Monde*'s front-page said that psychologists would decide whether Reagan was sharing 'a statement of repressed desire or the exorcism of a dreaded phantom'.[6] The Russian press also condemned it as 'invective, unprecedentedly hostile toward the Soviet Union and dangerous to the cause of peace'.[7] This study argues that 1984 should be remembered for much more than this off-script

INTRODUCTION 3

remark. The year is significant for the making of Reagan's legacy and his impact on American politics and culture. There are three central claims, which will in turn be discussed in depth below.

First, 1984 saw the consolidation of Reaganism in American politics and policy-making for a generation. Until Donald Trump's capture of the Republican Party, Reagan was the idol of the Grand Old Party and his political victories ensured that his shadow loomed over the Democrats too, particularly during the Clinton era. 1984 saw the culmination and consolidation of Reaganism in American life. Moreover, it also saw the beginnings of his second term's greatest failure (the Iran-Contra Affair) and pointed to his successful relationship with Mikhail Gorbachev (Soviet Premier, 1985–1991), which arguably saved his presidency in light of Iran-Contra. In short, the Reagan administration effectively traded arms to Iran in order to secure the release of hostages, with the funds then being diverted to the Contras via secret bank accounts.[8]

Second, it was by winning re-election, Reagan's impact on American life was undoubted and it was becoming clear that Reaganism permeated through popular culture. Indeed, even the movie *Ghostbusters*—released in 1984 but filmed earlier during Reagan's first term—saw free market economics as part of the ghost-hunting business. Reagan was perhaps the most media aware president the country had ever known. A product of the Warner studio system in the 1930s, former Screen Actors Guild president (1947–1952), and a lifelong movie devotee, Reagan understood how to handle a camera. He found himself fortieth president of the United States in a decade that was still captivated by the movies, hooked on television and engrossed in 'pop' music. Facts were the dominion of newspapers and radio reporters, not freely verifiable with the click of a mouse, while the focus of society turned inward and it was branded the 'me decade'.[9] Likewise, following a decade defined by memories of Vietnam, Watergate, and economic stagnation, many Americans seemed to turn away from the liberal consensus.[10] That the 1984 presidential election campaign was essentially fought as a personality contest allowed Reagan's team to play to his strengths: as a media personality, with a media blurring any distinction between life and art. The G.O.P. once again had a trained actor, and, after all, the nightly news had evolved into another form of entertainment, with poll numbers treated as television ratings. The American presidency had become a scripted performance, with props and settings in support of the protagonist.[11] It is for this world of a constructed presidency that Reagan was perfectly suited. Though

4   J. COOPER ET AL.

providing a full barometer of the country's mood in 1984 is beyond the scope of this study, consideration of key media released that year will be considered. Media that will be drawn upon include the highest grossing U.S. box-office movies, and the bestselling singles and albums, therefore capturing a sense of what the American public were choosing to spend time and money on, in order to gain some sense of the mood of the country. Knowing how carefully Reagan kept up with the movies, it makes sense to look back across the year to consider how media may have fed into the campaign or how the media reflected Regan through its mirror back to him.[12] Exploring this back and forth may shed new light on Reagan's success in winning his second term beyond the usual statistical assessment—and further demonstrate why 1984 was such a pivotal year for Reagan's legacy.[13] Reagan influenced his times as much as the times influenced Reagan.[14] Indeed, popular culture celebrated masculinity, individualism, and entrepreneurialism. Reagan and American culture were in response to the apparent decline of the 1970s, with the political climate influence popular culture, while the cultural shift celebrated and enforced the ideas of Reaganism.[15] As will be discussed below, Reagan was condemned in rap music, reflecting a majority view among African-Americans that he had failed to advance civil rights. While Reagan was not personally racist, his rhetoric on welfare conflated with racial imagery, such as his 1976 claims about the 'Chicago welfare queen', while he was blind to the impact of Reaganomics on African-Americans and his administration simply did not prioritise civil rights.[16] Perhaps it is therefore unsurprising that Reagan enjoyed the support of only 13% of African-American voters in 1980 (with even conservative third-party candidate, John Anderson, receiving 8% of the African-American vote).[17]

Third, it is in 1984 that it becomes clear how Reagan has both altered the office of the presidency, reversing its downgrading since the Ford and Carter years, and altered the course of the Cold War. During his first term, the tensions of the Cold War had reached heights not seen since the 1960s. Early in what proved to be the final decade of the Cold War, Reagan's rhetoric helped to increase the temperature. However, in 1984, Reagan began to move towards more conciliatory policies and rhetoric.[18] Therefore, it was in and around 1984 that the most heighted tensions of the Cold War, in many ways, ended forever since the Cold War itself ended five years later with the fall of the Berlin Wall. In between 1984 and 1989, the American president and the Soviet general secretary engaged each other in diplomacy more so than any two previously had

INTRODUCTION 5

done. Moreover, in February 1984, Yuri Andropov, the General Secretary of the Communist Party of the Soviet Union, died—after having succeeded Leonid Brezhnev (General Secretary, 1964–1982) who had died two years previously. Konstantin Chernenko, in turn, succeeded Andropov. Just a year later, Chernenko would die and be succeeded by Gorbachev. Reagan was not being disingenuous when he claimed that he had been unable to maintain a dialogue with his Soviet counterparts because 'they keep dying on me'.[19] 1984 was, therefore, the final year of the gerontocratic nature of Soviet leadership, but also the final year in which recalcitrance truly defined bilateral relations between the two superpowers.

The importance of the year 1984 is also crucial for another reason: Reagan's legacy upon the institution of the presidency itself. Throughout the 1970s, the U.S. presidency was in a relatively precarious position with regard to its authority to dominate the conduct of foreign policy. In 1981, the year during which Ronald Reagan assumed the office of the presidency, James Sundquist wrote the *Decline and Resurgence of Congress*, in which he argued that Congress—during the 1970s—had recaptured powers and responsibilities that it had surrendered to the presidency in recent decades.[20] The presidency's usurpation and abuse of certain constitutional powers were brought to the forefront during the Nixon presidency and subsequent Watergate scandal, which, in turn, led to Congress' reassertion of its authority over certain issues such as the conduct of intelligence operations and the employment of the war power.[21] Consequently, scholars, throughout the 1970s, spoke about the president's monopoly over the direction of foreign policy and other expansive executive credos, such as executive privilege, which were often invoked by Richard Nixon during the Watergate investigation.[22] In turn, the resurgence of congress, during the 1970s, occurred through the passage of legislation that sought to curtail the power of the presidency and 'aimed to limit the autonomy of executive branch law enforcement and intelligence activities at home and abroad'.[23] Even before Reagan was elected president, he sought to fight back against what he perceived to have been the imposition of a newly dominant legislative paradigm vis-a-vis foreign policy. For instance, Reagan, during a Lincoln Day dinner speech in February 1980, declared that the Central Intelligence Agency (CIA) 'should be allowed to pursue covert activities without congressional restraints' and that, 'We must once again restore the U.S. intelligence community. Senseless restrictions requiring the CIA to report any and all covert actions to eight congressional committees must be eliminated'.[24] This foreshadowed Reagan's desire to reassert the power and authority of the presidency, and executive branch writ large, in executing foreign policy. The fact that Reagan won a landslide victory in the 1984 presidential election can be seen as evidence that his reassertion of presidential power was successful especially with commentary during that year declaring that the presidency works. Voters saw Reagan as a strong leader who was able to get things done despite opposition from other branches of government.

In November 2011, the Pew Research Center published an analysis about the political views of different generations in the United States, namely the 'silent' generation (born 1928 to 1945), baby boomers (born 1946 to 1964), generation X (born 1965 to 1980), and millennials (born 1981 to 1993).[25] For older Americans, Reagan is viewed in high regard. The silent generation cite Reagan as the best president in their lifetime (36% of support) and baby boomers agree (with 33% saying he is in first place, and 12% in second place). Both generations also have high regard for Bill Clinton—27% of baby boomers say he was the best president in their lifetime, along with 35% of the 'silent' generation.[26] Reagan's post-presidential approval has been impressive. In March 2002, 73% of Americans approved of his job performance, with only President John F. Kennedy ranked higher at 83%. In November 2003, Reagan was ranked third (behind Kennedy and Lincoln) in an opinion poll asking about the greatest U.S. president. Reagan fares better in memory than during his administration. He averaged a 53% job approval rating—higher than Richard Nixon, Gerald Ford, and Jimmy Carter, but lower than his immediate successors, George H.W. Bush and Clinton. In 1981, Reagan enjoyed a job approval of 60% in March (increasing to 68% in May after he was shot by John Hinckley, Jr.) but by the end of the year, this number had declined to 49%. Reagan's second year as president saw his approval remain in the 40% bracket, ending 1982 at 41% and seeing the Republicans lose 25 seats in the House of Representatives during the midterm elections. Even though Reagan was scored at 35% for job approval at the beginning of 1983, that figure increased to 50% by November that year and remained above that up to and including the 1984 general election (Reagan's job approval in October 1984 was 58%). Support for Reagan remained high as his second term began, with a high of 68% in May 1986. However, the Iran-Contra scandal dented his support, with a dramatic dop to 47% approval in December 1986. Approval for

Reagan's performance would increase piecemeal, allowing him to close his presidency with an approval of 57% in November 1988 and 63% the following month. Of course, approval for Reagan's job performance when measured during his time in office should be mapped to the successes of his administration at the time. For instance, the successful intervention in Grenada—following the Beirut bombing—coincided with the increase in support for Reagan in November 1983.[27] Similarly, the performance of the American economy shaped Reagan's approval ratings, particularly during his first term. Unemployment increased from 7.5% to 8.6% between January 1981 and January 1982. The end of Reagan's second year in the White House saw unemployment at almost 11%. The upturn in Reagan's approval ratings at the end of 1983 coincided with an improved performance on employment, with unemployment declining to 8.3% and then to 7.2% in time for Reagan's re-election. This downward trajectory for unemployment in the United States would fall to less than 6% in September 1987.[28]

Assessment about Reagan's impact on the United States can be eclectic and difficult to pin down. For instance, one of the president's many famous quotes was, 'The nine most terrifying words in the English language are: I'm from the Government, and I'm here to help'.[29] However, the notion of 'trust' in government among Americans actually rebounded during his administration. In March 1980, at the nadir of the Jimmy Carter administration (1977–1981), only 27% of Americans believed that the government could be trusted to dop the right thing always or most of the time. This increased under Reagan, with a high of 45% in February 1985, and not dropping below 40%, even in the wake of the Iran-Contra revelations.[30] The contradictions about Reagan's record were evident in the tentative conclusions of leading presidential biographers and historians, when asked to comment by the Hoover Institution in April 1989. Responses broadly concurred that Reagan's rhetoric and tax cuts would be a lasting legacy that would shape the future of both the Republicans and the Democrats. Likewise, his articulation of the 'American dream' and national self-confidence was a welcome boon to a country in need of uplifting following the 1970s' challenges of Watergate, the Vietnam War, and economic difficulties. However, the U.S. budgetary deficit, inequalities, and an uncertain legacy in foreign affairs (where Reagan ostensibly moved from Cold Warrior to enthusiastic peace negotiator) were among the negatives on the Reagan ledger.[31] The advent of the Reagan era represented a break with the economic and political consensus that has characterised the United States since the 1930s. The United States government essentially sought to mitigate the worst effects of capitalism through programmes such as the New Deal and aspects of the Great Society. The role of the federal government in American life was challenged by Reagan's policies and, perhaps even more importantly, in the longer term, by his rhetoric.[32] Re-election in 1984 meant that Reagan's impact on the American economic and political system was ensured. For instance, Reagan's rhetoric meant that low taxation became an article of faith for Republicans regardless of the fiscal consequences, in what Iwan Morgan described as the 'age of deficits' from the Carter administration to the George W. Bush administration.[33]

Reaganism focused on two key components: reduce the role and influence of government in the United States, and win a global battle of ideas, between capitalism and liberal democracy, compared with communism as espoused by the Soviet Union. In turn, Reaganomics saw federal tax cuts at marginal rates and a dramatic escalation in rhetoric and military build-up in the Cold War. In economics, Reagan adopted supply-side policies, and successfully navigated passed a Democrat-controlled House of Representatives and ensured the Republican-controlled Senate's support for the 1981 Economic Recovery Tax Act, which over three years reduced marginal income taxation from 70% to 50%. The economist supply-siders, led by Arthur Laffer and his famous 'Laffer Curve', argued that lower taxes would increase incentives and productivity, which would create more economic growth, which would mean that the tax cuts would pay for themselves. Reagan's 1986 Tax Reform Act simplified the federal tax code by moving it from four tax brackets to two (at 15 and 28%).[34] Reagan's tax cuts, alongside the increase in military spending and a reluctance to significantly reduce spending led to an increasing U.S. budgetary deficit. In 1982, so-called entitlements, for instance social security, were worth 48% of the federal budget. Moreover, defence spending was 25% of the budget, with a further 10% allocated to servicing the national debt. As such, the politicians in Washington, D.C. were politically reluctant to touch approximately 85% of the federal budget. The Reagan administration would see the U.S. national debt nearly triple to $2.7 trillion.[35] There were bipartisan agreements to mitigate the deficit with higher corporate taxes, which Reagan signed into law as the 1982 Tax Equity and Fiscal Responsibility Act and 1984 Deficit Reduction Act. While Reagan and Congress jostled over fiscal policy, monetary policy was the purview of Paul Volcker, Chairman of the Federal Reserve (1979–1987). Volcker's 'monetary-based control' leads to high interest rates. Nonetheless, Volcker would move away from tight monetarist policy, meaning that after 1982—where the Republicans' fortunes in the House of Representatives were reversed from the gains on Reagan's coat tails in 1980, to losses amid the Reagan recession—the economic outlook began to improve.[36]

Despite Reagan's best efforts to convince the American public about the dangers posed by the Soviet Union, they remained cautious about increasing military spending in the context of the rising U.S. budgetary deficit. In September 1983, only one in four Americans were unconcerned about the deficit, while 78% opposed raising taxes and 82% opposed reducing entitlements as a means to address this. In contrast, 55% believed that reduced defence spending was the best means to tackle it.[37] Reagan had to make the case for increasing defence spending in clearer terms, and his speech introducing the concept of the Strategic Defence Initiative and the importance of a strong military to prevent war, saw a shift in his rhetoric in time for the 1984 election campaign.[38]

In foreign affairs, Reagan's first term had focused on restoring a sense of lost national prestige following the Carter years. The administration's 1981–1982 sanctions against the Soviet Union, with a particular focus on the Soviet Gas-Pipe to Western Europe, angered his allies, even the closest in Margaret Thatcher (the UK prime minister, 1979–1990), who saw their own domestic economic interests undermined by Reagan's Cold Warrior positioning. Although these sanctions were eased by the end of his second year in the White House, Reagan's stance towards the Soviet Union was unyielding. At his Westminster address in June 1982 to the British Parliament, the president called upon allies to join him in a crusade, a battle of ideas, which would see Marxist-Leninism consigned to 'the ash-heap of history'.[39] For Reagan, the Cold War would be won and the bi-polar world of East and West was not a permanent status quo. However, this optimistic call to arms was concurrent to Reagan's fierce condemnation of the United States' geo-political opponents. For instance, in his 1983 address to the National Association of Evangelical Christians, Reagan recalled:

> A number of years ago, I heard a young father, a very prominent young man in the entertainment world, addressing a tremendous gathering in California. It was during the time of the cold war, and communism and our own way of life were very much on people's minds. And he was speaking

10 J. COOPER ET AL.

to that subject. And suddenly, though, I heard him saying, "I love my little girls more than anything -- --"' And I said to myself, "Oh, no, don't. You can't -- don't say that." But I had underestimated him. He went on: "I would rather see my little girls die now, still believing in God, than have them grow up under communism and one day die no longer believing in God."[40]

Reagan famously continued, 'I urge you to beware the temptation of pride -- the temptation of blithely declaring yourselves above it all and label both sides equally at fault, to ignore the facts of history and the aggressive impulses of an evil empire, to simply call the arms race a giant misunderstanding and thereby remove yourself from the struggle between right and wrong and good and evil'.[41] When pressed about this rhetoric by the *New York Times*, Thatcher defended Reagan's 'evil empire' comment on the basis that it 'was much deeper' than a line for 'domestic consumption'. She said, 'Ron Reagan and I think very much the same way; because I had come to the same conclusion'.[42] Nonetheless, in the same moment, she remarked:

> That in a very dangerous world the thing is not whether you agree with the other very powerful bloc's political views or not; the important thing is you simply must make an effort the more to understand one another. Secondly, if as the President wishes and as all Europe wishes, you want to get down the tremendous expenditure on armaments, then you can only do it if you both agree on it. You can only both agree on it if you do more talking to one another.[43]

Thatcher would prove to be both proponent and opponent of the decisions taken in Reagan's White House.[44] For instance, the prime minister lauded Reagan's Westminster address, but was furious about his decision to invade Grenada—a member of the British-led Commonwealth of Nations—in October 1983, despite his claims that it was at the request of the Organisation of East Caribbean States, and to rescue American medical students following the Marxist coup in the country.[45] Of course, Grenada can be viewed in the context of two aspects of Reagan's first term. The first is as an example of the Reagan Doctrine in action.[46] As he began to articulate within his 1982 speech at Westminster, advocating for the world's democracies to stand against the totalitarian aggression of the Soviet bloc—which Thatcher herself would declare as the manifesto of the Reagan Doctrine—the president wanted to 'rollback' global communism.[47] In January 1984, *The New York Times* stated that Reagan established a 'framework in which small wars might be fought to forestall bigger conflicts, or to "roll back" Soviet influence, as in Grenada, if the chance came along'.[48] Secondly, a rapid and successful military operation in Grenada was a welcome antidote to 'Vietnam syndrome', proving that the United States could win wars. Likewise, following the decision to withdraw American military personnel from Lebanon after the Beirut bombing that killed 241 Americans, the Reagan administration could also point to Grenada as a national security success rather than allowing protracted debates about the merits of a potentially more lengthy, costly, and complex action in the Middle East.[49] A third consideration is perhaps more cynical. A successful and brief war would be a welcome boon to Reagan's re-election campaign in 1984.[50]

The increasing availability of documentary material at the Ronald Reagan Presidential Library, concurrent to oral histories and the availability of members of the Reagan administration, has seen an upswing in scholarly works about Reagan's presidency. Works from eminent historians have arguably overtaken biographical accounts of Reagan's life and career, which may be described as examples of 'higher journalism'.[51] Similarly, the works of scholars utilising declassified materials have strengthened the literature about Reagan's foreign policy, many of which are classic texts.[52] The possibilities and potential for future research endeavours related to the Reagan years are also evident in the variety of topics and approaches undertaken by historians and presidential scholars.[53] For this study's purposes, 1984 is recognised by Aaron Donaghy's seminal work as a key year in the final stages of the Cold War. Reagan's fourth year in office saw a change in his approach towards the Soviet Union. The president was mortified by even the notion of a nuclear war. This instinct, coupled with polling that showed he needed to talk more about 'peace' than 'strength' in order to win re-election, saw Reagan abandon his hard-line approach and embrace the politics of pragmatism.[54] Similarly, William Inboden has argued that the ending of the Cold War is more attributable to Reagan's political abilities and instincts, including during his first term, as opposed to decisions made in the Kremlin.[55] Sarah Thomson explored the president's re-election campaign, specifically the use of his European tour in June 1984 as an extension of the classic 'rose garden strategy', with nuance.[56] Likewise, scholars are turning their attention to the process and significance of creating presidential legacies. This process can involve success at home and abroad, the work of White House staff, presidential libraries, major speeches (particularly farewell addresses), impact on popular culture and creative arts, and the marking of significance anniversaries.[57] Indeed, that at the time of writing we are close to 2024 has not been lost on this study's authors. 2024 will be another U.S. presidential election year, but also forty years since Reagan's landslide victory. Comparisons between the fortieth president and the Republican nominee, and the oldest incumbent president, will likely abound.

The role of collective memory—meaning the how and why—Reagan is remembered is worthy of further study, and not just because of a looming fortieth anniversary. Reagan is still viewed in the highest regard among many people in the United States. In 2018, an opinion poll saw Kennedy, Reagan, and Obama rated as the best of White House occupants since the 1950s.[58] A 2021 survey showed that 42% of Republicans view Reagan as the most effective president during the last forty years, with 23% of all voters choosing Reagan (only President Barack Obama was higher with 35% support).[59] Scholars' interest in the Reagan years is still likely some time away from reaching a zenith. In the meantime, it is the central claim of this work that a crossover between both popular and academic understanding correlates around 1984.[60] This singular year saw Reagan re-elected to even higher support than his victory over Jimmy Carter in 1980. For Reaganites, it also saw the consolidation of economic recovery and beginning of economic growth in the United States. Moreover, 1984 was the year that Reagan's approach to the Cold War explicitly changed gears and the world learnt that *Star Wars* was not just an already iconic science fiction franchise, but also the Strategic Defence Initiative, a yet-to-be-realised emblem of the president's calls for a world without nuclear weapons. This study contributes to collective scholastic efforts to move towards a history of the Reagan administration—and it does so by exploring the importance and impact of Ronald Reagan's 1984.

NOTES

1. See, for instance: *C-SPAN*, 'Presidential Historians Survey 2001': https://www.c-span.org/presidentsurvey2021/?page=overall. [Hereafter simply the URL for when sources accessed this way.]
2. H. W. Brands: 'What Makes a President Great,' Hauenstein Center, 2013: https://www.youtube.com/watch?v=f_CYPKdc6EI. I am

INTRODUCTION   13

grateful to Professor Brands for allowing me to use his idea in this work. For the 2012 U.S. presidential election results, see: https://www.nytimes.com/elections/2012/results/president.html.

3. George Orwell, *Nineteen Eighty-Four* (London: Penguin Classics, 2021).

4. Reagan's Joke Lead To Red Alert | Flashback | *NBC News*: https://www.youtube.com/watch?v=CFCABnWlN8E. See also: 'Reagan Said to Joke of Bombing Russia Before Radio Speech,' *The New York Times*, 13 August 1984, A16.

5. Fay S. Joyce, 'Mondale Chides Reagan on Soviet- Bombing Joke,' *The New York Times*, 14 August 1984, A20.

6. From *Le Monde*, quoted in the *New York Times*, 14 August 1984, A8: https://timesmachine.nytimes.com/timesmachine/1984/08/14/132752.html?pageNumber=8.

7. Celestine Bohlen, 'Soviets formally denounce Reagan's Joke,' *The Washington Post*, 16 August 1984, accessed via: www.washingtonpost.com/archive/politics/1984/08/16/soviets-formally-denounce-reagans-joke/3d93b376-56f8-4791-bc64-3c1459227ac3/.

8. For an excellent summary of this affair, please see: Kyle Longley, 'An Obsession: The Central American Policy of the Reagan Administration,' in Bradley Lynn Coleman and Kyle Longley (eds.), *Reagan and the World: Leadership and National Security, 1981–1989* (Lexington, KY: University Press of Kentucky, 2017), 220–227. The classic work about Iran-Contra remains: Malcolm Byrne, *Iran-Contra: Reagan's Scandal and the Unchecked Abuse of Presidential Power* (Lawrence, KS: University Press of Kansas, 2014).

9. Tom Wolfe, 'The 'Me' Decade and the Third Great Awakening,' *New York Magazine*, 23 August 1976, accessed via: nymag.com/news/features/45938/.

10. Randall B. Woods, *Quest for Identity: America Since 1945*, Cambridge: Cambridge University Press, 2005), 443.

11. D. Peberdy, *Masculinity and Film Performance: Male Angst in Contemporary American Cinema* (London: Palgrave, 2011), 25.

12. Susan Jeffords, *Hard Bodies: Hollywood Masculinity in the Reagan Era* (New Brunswick, NJ: Rutgers University Press, 1994), 4.

13. For the use of film as historical sources, see, for instance: Paul B. Weinstein, 'Movies as the Gateway to History: The History and Film Project,' *The History Teacher* 35:1 (2001), 27–48. For using music in this way, see, for instance: Shirli Gilbert, 'Music

14   J. COOPER ET AL.

as Historical Source: Social History and Musical Texts,' *International Review of the Aesthetics and Sociology of Music* 36:1 (2005), 117–134.

14. This approach has been used to great success in David S. Reynolds' seminar work: *Abe: Abraham Lincoln in His Times* (New York: Penguin Press, 2020). For Reynolds, 'Cultural biography reveals not only *self-making* but also *culture-making*. Culture fashioned Lincoln; in turn he fashioned it (p. xvii).'

15. See, for instance, this classic text: Jeffords, *Hard Bodies*.

16. Iwan Morgan, *Reagan: American Icon* (London: I.B. Tauris, 2016), 241–242. For a contrasting—and damning—view about Reagan's attitude towards race and its longer-term impact on the Republican Party and U.S. politics, see: Daniel S. Lucks, *Reconsidering Reagan: Racism, Republicans, and the Road to Trump* (Boston, MA: Beacon Press, 2020). For how American social attitudes towards race developed during the Reagan era, and its relationship with policy-making and politicking, see: John Kenneth White, *Barack Obama's America: How New Conceptions of Race, Family, and Religion Ended the Reagan Era* (Ann Arbor, MI: University of Michigan Press, 2009).

17. 'How Groups Voted in 1980,' *Roper Center for Public Opinion Research*: https://ropercenter.cornell.edu/how-groups-voted-1980. [Hereafter Roper Center.]

18. M. V. Paulauskas, 'Reagan, the Soviet Union, and the Cold War, 1981–1985,' in Andrew L. Johns (ed.), *A Companion to Ronald Reagan* (Oxford: Oxford University Press, 2015), 277.

19. Ronald Reagan, *An American Life: The Autobiography* (New York, NY: Simon and Schuster, 1990), 611.

20. J. L. Sundquist, *The Decline and Resurgence of Congress* (Washington, D.C.: Brookings Institution, 1981).

21. See: Douglas Brinkley and Luke Nichter, *The Nixon Tapes: 1973* (New York, NY: Houghton Mifflin, 2015); A. Schlesinger, *The Imperial Presidency* (Boston, MA: Houghton Mifflin, 1973).

22. See, for instance: Raoul Berger, *Executive Privilege: A Constitutional Myth* (Cambridge, MA: Harvard University Press, 1974); Raoul Berger, 'The Presidential Monopoly of Foreign Relations,' *Michigan Law Review* 71:1 (1972), 1–58.

23. A. Rudalevige. *The New Imperial Presidency: Renewing Presidential Power after Watergate* (Ann Arbor, MI: University of

Michigan Press, 2005), 7; John Yoo, *Crisis and Command: A History of Executive Power from George Washington to George W. Bush* (New York, NY: Kaplan, 2011), 73: Such statutes included the 1972 Case-Zablocki Act which was to ensure Congress was kept informed about international commitments made by executive agreements; the 1973 War Powers Resolution which sought to delimit the president's authority to authorise force unilaterally; the 1974 Hughes-Ryan Amendment which put into statute new reporting requirements that demanded that the CIA must brief eight committees on the justification for covert actions underway; the National Emergencies Act of 1976 terminated existing national emergencies and required the president to make certain findings before declaring a new one; the 1978 Foreign Intelligence Surveillance Act required a warrant from a federal court before an electronic surveillance measure could be authorised; and the 1980 Intelligence Oversight Act which sought to regulate the president's control over covert operations.

24. Lou Cannon, 'Reagan's Foreign Policy: Scrap "Weakness, Illusion," Stress Military Strength,' *Washington Post*, 16 February 1980: https://www.washingtonpost.com/archive/politics/1980/02/16/reagans-foreign-policy-scrap-weakness-illusion-stress-military-strength/f95da6f5-62b9-4b52-b320-8e5ac0e08d4f/.

25. *Pew Research Center*, 'The Generation Gap and the 2012 Election,' 3 November 2011: https://www.pewresearch.org/politics/2011/11/03/the-generation-gap-and-the-2012-election-3/.

26. Ibid.

27. Frank Newport, Jeffrey M. Jones and Lydia Saad, 'Ronald Reagan From the People's Perspective: A Gallup Poll Review,' 7 June 2004: https://news.gallup.com/poll/11887/ronald-reagan-from-peoples-perspective-gallup-poll-review.aspx.

28. Tom Rosentiel, 'It's All About Jobs, Except When It's Not: Unemployment and Presidential Approval Ratings 1981–2009,' Pew Research Center, 26 January 2010: https://www.pewresearch.org/2010/01/26/its-all-about-jobs-except-when-its-not/.

29. Ronald Reagan, News Conference, 12 August 1986: https://www.reaganfoundation.org/ronald-reagan/reagan-quotes-speeches/news-conference-1/.

30. Feature, 'Public Trust in Government: 1958–2022,' *Pew Research Center*, 6 June 2022: https://www.pewresearch.org/politics/2022/06/06/public-trust-in-government-1958-2022/.
31. Stephen E. Ambrose, M. E. Bradford, Alonzo L. Hamby, Forrest McDonald, George H. Nash, James Nuechterlein, and Karl O'Lessker, 'Our 40th President's Place in History,' *Hoover Institution*, 1 April 1989: https://www.hoover.org/research/how-great-was-ronald-reagan.
32. For classic examples of the historiography on this issue, see: Gary Gerstle, *The Rise and Fall of the Neoliberal Order: America and the World in the Free Market Era* (Oxford: Oxford University Press, 2022); and, Sean Willentz, *The Age of Reagan: A History, 1974-2008* (New York, NY: Harper, 2008).
33. For this seminal work, see: Iwan Morgan, *The Age of Deficits: Presidents and Unbalanced Budgets from Jimmy Carter to George W. Bush* (Lawrence, KS: University Press of Kansas, 2009).
34. For an introduction to Reaganomics, see, for instance, James H. Broussard, *Ronald Reagan: Champion of conservative America* (London: Routledge, 2015), 117–122, 135–137. For a wider discussion about the development and implementation of supply-side economics, see: Brian Domitrovic, *Econoclasts: The Rebels Who Sparked the Supply-Side Revolution and Restored American Prosperity* (Wilmington, DE: ISI Books, 2009), 203–252.
35. Michael Schaller, *Reckoning with Reagan: American and Its President in the 1980s* (Oxford: Oxford University Press, 1992), 45–46.
36. James Cooper, *Margaret Thatcher and Ronald Reagan: A Very Political Special Relationship* (Basingstoke: Palgrave, 2012), 31, 63–66, 67–70.
37. Richard C. Auxier, Researcher/Editorial Assistant, *Pew Research Center*, 'Reagan's Recession,' Pew Research Center, 14 December 2010: https://www.pewresearch.org/2010/12/14/reagans-recession/.
38. Ronald Reagan, 'Address to the Nation on Defense and National Security,' 23 March 1983: https://www.reaganlibrary.gov/archives/speech/address-nation-defense-and-national-security.
39. Ronald Reagan, 'Address to Members of the British Parliament,' 8 June 1982: https://www.reaganlibrary.gov/archives/speech/address-members-british-parliament.

40. Ronald Reagan, 'Remarks at the annual convention of the National Association of Evangelicals in Orland, Florida,' 8 March 1983: https://www.reaganfoundation.org/library-museum/permanent-exhibitions/berlin-wall/from-the-archives/remarks-at-the-annual-convention-of-the-national-association-of-evangelicals-in-orlando-florida/.
41. Ibid.
42. Margaret Thatcher, Interview for *New York Times*, 20 January 1984: https://www.margaretthatcher.org/document/105520.
43. Ibid.
44. See, for instance, Richard Aldous, *Reagan and Thatcher: The Difficult Relationship* (London: Hutchinson, 2012); and James Cooper, *A Diplomatic Meeting: Reagan, Thatcher, and the Art of Summitry* (Lexington, KY: University Press of Kentucky, 2022).
45. Cooper, *Diplomatic Meeting*, 93–96, 121–127.
46. W. R. Bode, 'The Reagan Doctrine,' in United States Strategic Institute,' *Strategic Review, Volume 14.* (Washington, D.C., 1986), 21–22.
47. Charles Krauthammer, 'Essay: The Reagan Doctrine,' *Time*, 1 April 1985: http://content.time.com/time/subscriber/article/0,33009,964873,00.html. Krauthammer wrote, after Reagan's 1985 State of the Union speech, that Reagan 'has produced the Reagan Doctrine…The Reagan Doctrine proclaims overt and unashamed American support for anti-Communist revolution. The grounds are justice, necessity, and democratic tradition.' Margaret Thatcher, *The Downing Street Years* (London: Harper Collins, 1993), 258: Thatcher wrote about the 1982 Westminster speech that the 'speech itself was a remarkable one. It marked a decisive stage in the battle of ideas which he and I wished to wage against socialism, above all the socialism of the Soviet Union…In his speech President Reagan proposed a worldwide campaign for democracy to support the "democratic revolution which was gathering new strength…" It was the manifesto of the Reagan doctrine'.
48. Richard Halloran, 'Reagan as Military Commander,' *The New York Times*, 15 January 1984: https://www.nytimes.com/1984/01/15/magazine/reagan-as-military-commander.html.
49. See, for instance: H.W. Brands, *Reagan: The Life* (New York, NY: Doubleday, 2015), 395–403.

50. L. Gelb, 'Is the Nuclear Threat Manageable?' *The New York Times*, 4 March 1984: https://www.nytimes.com/1984/03/04/magazine/is-the-nuclear-threat-manageable.html.

51. Higher journalistic works include: Lou Cannon, *President Reagan: The Role of a Lifetime* (New York: Simon & Schuster, 1991) and George Wills, *Reagan's America: Innocents at Home* (London: Heinemann, 1988). Excellent academic biographies include: Brands, *Reagan*, and Iwan Morgan, *Reagan: American Icon* (London: I.B. Taurus, 2016).

52. See, for instance: Beth Fischer, *The Reagan Reversal: Foreign Policy and the End of the Cold War* (Columbia, MO: University of Missouri Press, 1997). More recent examples, utilising the declassified materials and adding to a broader scholarship about grand strategy, include: James Wilson, *The Triumph of Improvisation: Gorbachev's Adaptability, Reagan's Engagement, and the End of the Cold War* (Ithaca: Cornell University Press, 2015), and Simon Miles, *Engaging the Evil Empire Washington, Moscow, and the Beginning of the End of the Cold War* (Ithaca: Cornell University Press, 2020). For a discussion about grand strategy, see: Nina Silove, 'Beyond the Buzzword: The Three Meanings of "Grand Strategy",' *Security Studies* 27:1 (2018), 27–57.

53. See, for instance: *Malcolm Byrne, Iran-Contra: Reagan's Scandal and the Unchecked Abuse of Presidential Power* (Lawrence, KS: University Press of Kansas, 2014); Doug Rossinow, *The Reagan Era: A History of the 1980s* (New York, NY: Columbia University Press, 2015); Andrew L. Johns (ed.), *A Companion to Ronald Reagan* (Malden, MA: Wiley Blackwell, 2015); Bradley Lynn Coleman and Kyle Longley (eds.), *Reagan and the World: Leadership and National Security, 1981–1989* (Lexington, KY: University Press of Kentucky, 2017); and, Cooper, *A Diplomatic Meeting*.

54. Aaron Donaghy, *The Second Cold War: Carter, Reagan, and the Politics of Foreign Policy* (Cambridge: Cambridge University Press, 2021), 1–17.

55. For this masterful and authoritative account of Reagan's approach to the Cold War and other foreign policy issues and events, see: William Inboden, *The Peacemaker: Ronald Reagan, the Cold War, and the World on the Brink* (New York, NY: Dutton, 2022).

56. S. M. G. Thomson, 'Presidential Travel and the Rose Garden Strategy: A Case Study of Ronald Reagan's 1984 Tour of Europe,' *Presidential Studies Quarterly*, 50 (2020), 864–888.
57. Michael Patrick Cullinane and Sylvia Ellis (eds.), *Constructing Presidential Legacy: How We Remember the American President* (Edinburgh: Edinburgh University Press, 2018).
58. *UVA Center for Politics*, 'Public Rates Presidents: Kennedy, Reagan, Obama at Top, Nixon, Johnson, Trump at Bottom,' 15 February 2018: https://centerforpolitics.org/crystalball/articles/public-rates-presidents-jfk-reagan-obama-at-top-nixon-lbj-trump-at-bottom/.
59. Amina Dunn, 'Republicans view Reagan, Trump as best recent presidents,' *Pew Research Center*, 20 December 2021: https://www.pewresearch.org/fact-tank/2021/12/20/republicans-view-reagan-trump-as-best-recent-presidents/.
60. For an outstanding example of the tracing of the use of presidential memory, see: Michael Patrick Cullinane, *Theodore Roosevelt's Ghost: The History and Memory of an American Icon* (Baton Rouge: Louisiana State University Press, 2017); K. Longley, J. D. Mayer, M. Schaller, and J. W. Sloan (eds.), *Deconstructing Reagan: Conservative Mythology and America's Fortieth President.* (New York, 2007).

1984

Abstract This central chapter offers a commentary and analysis of Ronald Reagan's re-election campaign. It does so by locating the election campaign, its key themes and events, within the broader context of U.S. and international politics. In addition, the campaign is contextualised by an exploration of popular culture, specifically movies and music. The contradictions between Reagan's optimistic message about the United States and the reality of economic and social inequalities are explored. The chapter shows that the successes and controversies associated with the Reagan years correlate around the year 1984.

Keywords Reaganomics · Campaign strategy · Republicans · Democrats · Popular culture

LOOKING AHEAD TO RE-ELECTION

As part of an audit about how the president's time was organised, Michael Deaver (White House deputy chief of staff, 1981–1985) noted that, in 1984, Reagan spent around 25% of his time with his national security team, but, by September, half of his time dedicated to political matters, with this increasing to 80% in October. The cabinet enjoyed 8% of Reagan's attention, whereas the press used a similar amount of his time.[1]

© The Author(s), under exclusive license to Springer Nature Switzerland AG 2024
J. Cooper et al., *Ronald Reagan's 1984*,
https://doi.org/10.1007/978-3-031-53677-9_2

22   J. COOPER ET AL.

That the president would spend so much time in any given year with the National Security Council is unsurprising. Likewise, the amount of time committed to re-election can be equally expected—after all, without a successful election night, Reagan would have had ample spare time after inauguration day in January 1985. The president's re-election—built on an improving economy and restored national prestige and aims of peace in the Cold War—saw a political campaign that has defined Reagan's presidency. It encompassed major speeches at home and abroad, policy developments, emphases on successes and hostages to fortune.

The 1982 midterms were held at the height of the 'Reagan recession', which only compounded the standard political cycle that saw the party that controlled the White House experience electoral defeat. With Reagan's approval rating at 42%, the elections saw the Republicans lose 26 seats in the U.S. House of Representatives.[2] Although the president's party held on to control of the U.S. Senate, the White House's legislative agenda was dramatically undermined. The Reagan administration has managed to work with conservative Democrats in Congress to pass its 1981 tax cuts through the Democrat-controlled House of Representatives, a larger majority for Reagan's opponents made a repeat of such a feat more challenging. The results turned the White House's attention to the 1984 election and the prospects of a second term for the president. Among the midterm's fallout was a report to Reagan from his pollster, Richard Wirthlin, in December 1982.[3] In an extensive briefing, Wirthlin argued:

> In 1981 we were successful in pushing through Congress many of our legislative programs. This ... has led to a landmark Administration that can alter the Presidential Agenda for the next two decades.
>
> However, the centrifugal forces that will disperse and dissipate your presidential power are enormous. We start 1983 less strong politically that we were in 1981. Only:
>
> - by focusing on the strengths of the general goals,
> - by dealing to the constituents we need to keep our grass roots support strong, and
> - by developing an issue agenda that will put us in a position to be of maximal advantage in 1983 can we properly prepare the ground for Republican successes in the 1984 election. But more importantly, only by doing these things in 1983 can we keep the Reagan Revolution alive for another two decades.[4]

1984 was, thus, viewed as both a significant election year and crucial for cementing Reagan's legacy and imprint as president. In the meantime, according to Wirthlin, Reagan would have to contend with expected political opposition from the Democrats and politicking by potential Republican presidential candidates, who would prepare themselves should Reagan choose not to seek re-election. Nonetheless, his overriding concern was to restore Reagan's 'perceptual strengths', such as his leadership qualities and empathy for the most vulnerable in society, and an electorally successful coalition, which would need to include women, Catholics, senior citizens, lower- and middle-income workers, southern conservative and moderates who ticket-split across both parties. To do this, Wirthlin emphasised the need, for instance, for economic growth, a balanced budget, fairness (particularly with regard to supporting and protecting social security), and a clear approach to arms reductions and a 'constructive summit' with the Soviet leadership.[5] Wirthlin's advice was echoed in an extensive report about the Reagan coalition.[6] It was expected that Reagan's supporters in 1984 would still include: high-income voters (including Catholics and union families), educated Southern Whites and Catholics, middle-class southern white and protestants in the north, soft support from young and non-union voters, and non-union men across the country (and Catholic). Reagan could expect to not have the support of African-Americans, non-union and less affluent northern Protestants and northern union voters with low or moderate incomes and college degrees. It was unclear about the political affiliation for the following: educated low northern protestants who had moderate incomes, middle aged and middle-class Catholic in the industrial Midwest, white protestants in the North-East, northern women, and poorer whites in the south. This latter grouping was to be targeted by the Reagan campaign. It was viewed as vital that the Reagan re-election campaign mitigated the issue of 'fairness'—this was a successful theme for the Democrats in the 1982 midterm elections.[7] The decision for the Reagan campaign to be essentially a centrist one, maximising imagery and emotion, rather than detailed policies represented a change in approach by the Republicans having learnt the political lessons in 1982. This was also seen in Reagan's preparations for his debates with Mondale. Ultimately, in 1984 Reagan enjoyed the support of 62% of men and 58% of women, 66% whites, every age group, and the majority of voters based on income. Mondale was more successful—in the breakdown of voter demographics—only among Democrats (74%), liberals (71%), African-Americans (91%), and Hispanics (66%) and Americans who earned less than \$12,500 a year (albeit only at 54% to Reagan's 46%).[8]

The Reagan campaign paid close attention to what had been Thatcher's successful re-election campaign earlier that year. Frank Fahrenkopf, the chairman of the Republican National Committee (RNC), welcomed a Conservative Party briefing about their success, and during the election itself, two RNC researchers, Anna Kondrates, an economist, and Vivienne Schneider, a foreign affairs expert, were based in the UK in order to observe the campaign. They wrote a full report, whereby they suggested that lessons could be learned for the forthcoming Republican campaign in 1984.[9] The report acknowledged that there were 'important differences in the American and British political contexts which make any direct and simple analogies misleading at best',[10] but it was apparent that:

> the incumbent must take the 'high road', emphasizing successes and turning the election into a referendum on "staying the course". The incumbent should take the offensive on potentially negative issues like unemployment, demonstrating concern and emphasizing that anyone who claims there are satisfactory short-term solutions is lying. The long-term connection between inflation and unemployment must be pounded into public consciousness.

Thatcher's successful war for the Falklands in 1982 enabled the conservatives to argue, 'British liberty and security would best be defended from a position of strength and through a demonstrated show of determination and resoluteness'. Moreover, Thatcher's resolute approach to leadership was 'a major conservative asset' ensuring that she was 'perceived as a decisive leader'. On the economy, Thatcher remained unwavering in her argument that unemployment would only be reduced by economic growth and, by refusing to 'stick her neck out with idle promises', she 'inspired confidence in a public happy to see real leadership at last'. The report argued that the president could enjoy similar success by showing a determination to 'stay the course'. Reagan was advised to adopt Thatcher's rhetoric, even if it was not necessarily for the same policy area: 'Like Ronald Reagan and Mrs. Thatcher, who repeatedly used the words "real jobs", Republicans in 1984 could use the term real peace'.[11] The 1983 Conservative campaign had contrasted Britain's economic performance in 1979, including images of the 'Winter of Discontent'. The

Reagan campaign would follow suit, particularly with regard to its television advertisements (as will be discussed below). In accordance with Reagan campaign's strategy, re-electing the president was presented to be key for an optimistic future. The campaigned ensured that Reagan and the G.O.P. owned the future, leaving the past to the Democrats.

The president's major shift towards 'peace' in the Cold War was marked with his explanation to the American people about his plans for the Strategic Defence Initiative (SDI) in March 1983. In a speech designed to cultivate wider support for increased defence spending, Reagan offered a new vision for the future: 'What if free people could live secure in the knowledge that their security did not rest upon the threat of instant U.S. retaliation to deter a Soviet attack, that we could intercept and destroy strategic ballistic missiles before they reached our own soil or that of our allies?'[12] He added that he was therefore 'directing a comprehensive and intensive effort to define a long-term research and development program to begin to achieve our ultimate goal of eliminating the threat posed by strategic nuclear missiles' on the basis that 'Our only purpose – one all people share – is to search for ways to reduce the danger of nuclear war'.[13] This initiative reversed the concept of mutually assured destruction (MAD) which was an understanding—held by both superpowers—that if one uses a nuclear weapon they would in turn have them used against them; it, therefore, acted as a deterrent. This caused much anxiety within the Soviet Union. Throughout this election year, then, SDI would be central to criticism of Reagan's leadership. For instance, the *Washington Post* argued, '"Star Wars" is bewilderingly complex' as it undone progress made in the previous decade, such as during the ABM treaty which limited the systems each side could build, and consequently 'Reagan has turned that logic upside down by suggesting that the United States may have the technical wherewithal to block the Soviets' best nuclear knockout punch, thus rendering impotent their offensive missiles'.[14]

1984 was one of Cold War's most complex years. On the one hand, it was becoming clear to many that Reagan's SDI not only sought to make the enemy's nuclear attack obsolete, but was guided—according to Donald T. Regan (who served as Reagan's Treasury Secretary, 1981–1985, and then his second White House Chief of Staff, 1985–1987)—by the idea 'of one day sitting down at the negotiating table with the leader of the U.S.S.R. and banning weapons of mass destruction from the planet'.[15] These themes were present throughout 1984. A *Washington Post* article, written by future Reagan biographer, Lou Cannon, claimed that the new Soviet premier, Andropov, welcomed Reagan's conciliatory remarks and for his call to renew U.S.-Soviet dialogue.[16] On the other hand, a 1984 memo to James Baker (White House Chief of Staff, 1981–1985, and then U.S. treasury secretary, 1985–1988) and Robert 'Bud' McFarlane (Reagan's national security adviser, 1983–1985), from Pamela J. Turner—Deputy Assistant to the President for Legislative Affairs—listed potential scenarios as to how the United States could 'most effectively assist Latin America and the Caribbean in democracy, economic improvement, and ability to resist outside aggression and subversion'.[17] Richard Armitage (assistant secretary of defence for international security affairs, 1983–1985) wrote to James Baker and Bud McFarlane: 'If a group is fighting a repressive regime and shares our values and our goals, then we have very little choice but to support them'.[18] Therefore, although strong Cold War rhetoric began to be eased in 1984, which was matched by Reagan's dedication to neutralising the threat of nuclear war through advocating arms reduction talks as well as proposing programmes such as SDI which would—on paper—have made a nuclear attack against the U.S. redundant, the Reagan administration was still dedicated to its mission of funding insurgents which was a policy being internally framed as an anti-Soviet measure.

Although SDI was a bold programme to announce, throughout the 1980s, and particularly throughout 1984, there was research undertaken by the American national security establishment regarding the potential impact of a nuclear winter. In early 1984, the Defense Nuclear Agency's Atmospheric Effects Division authored a now declassified document titled 'Global Effects of Nuclear War' in the attempt to develop a reasonable predictive capability and gauge the impacts on the climate and environment.[19] Interestingly, in February 1984, Reagan welcomed Neil Kinnock—the leader of the UK Labour Party (1983–1992)—to Washington, during which the former stressed his concerns about a nuclear war and how there could be no winner and widely discussed the notion of a nuclear winter.[20]

In an election year, everything is particularly political. Reagan used his incumbency to its full potential in key events throughout 1984. Even though he would not formally announce his candidacy for a second term until 29 January, the State of the Union on 25 January saw the president declare, 'America is Back with Four Great Goals'.[21] The president called for a national and bipartisan effort to achieve a balanced budget, lasting peace with the Soviet Union, a new frontier of space exploration and environmental protections, and support for families and children. The speech was littered with offers to different components of the Reagan coalition—support for school prayer, opposition to abortion, peace in the Cold War and across the world, tackling crime, improving education and opportunity, and advocating the private sector ahead of government spending and activities. Putting himself above politicking, yet in reality seeking to position himself in the centre-ground for the coming election, Reagan argued: 'When it comes to keeping America strong, free, and at peace, there should be no Republicans or Democrats, just patriotic Americans. We can decide the tough issues not by who is right, but by what is right'. Indeed, for the president, his first term was a cause for celebration and optimism:

> A rebirth of bipartisan cooperation, of economic growth, and military deterrence, and a growing spirit of unity among our people at home and our allies abroad underline a fundamental and far-reaching change: The United States is safer, stronger, and more secure in 1984 than before. We can now move with confidence to seize the opportunities for peace, and we will.[22]

A few days later, Reagan formally announced his intention to seek a second term:

> As I said Wednesday night, America is back and standing tall. We've begun to restore great American values -- the dignity of work, the warmth of family, the strength of neighborhood, and the nourishment of human freedom.
> But our work is not finished. We have more to do in creating jobs, achieving control over government spending, returning more autonomy to the States, keeping peace in a more settled world, and seeing if we can't find room in our schools for God.[23]

In a speech that unsurprisingly trumpets his record, Reagan used American history to capture the future for his campaign. Referring to Dr Joseph Warren (President of the Massachusetts Congress in 1775), Reagan stressed his compassion for all Americans:

28   J COOPER ET AL.

> We're here to lift the weak and to build the peace, and most important,
> we're here, as Dr. Warren said, to act today for the happiness and liberty
> of millions yet unborn, to seize the future so that every new child of this
> beloved Republic can dream heroic dreams. If we do less, we betray the
> memory of those who have given so much.[24]

In a further signal that he was determined to secure peace in the world,
Reagan achieved a nuclear agreement with China in April, which would
come into law in December 1985. If 1984 was Reagan seeking to recon-
cile America's past with an optimistic future, contingent to his re-election,
that year's Memorial Day commemorations afforded him the opportunity to tackle the Vietnam War and its legacy for the United States. On
28 May, Reagan spoke at Arlington National Cemetery what he called
'the national funeral for an unknown soldier who will today join the
heroes of three other wars'.[25] Noting the divisiveness about the conflict,
he remarked: 'We Americans have learned to listen to each other and to
trust each other again. We've learned that government owes the people an
explanation and needs their support for its actions at home and abroad.
And we have learned, and I pray this time for good, the most valuable
lesson of all -- the preciousness of human freedom'. The speech neatly
connected to Reagan's campaign themes of peace and optimism. Similarly, Reagan strengthened his bipartisanship credentials and mitigated
criticism about the U.S. deficit by signing into law the Deficit Reduction Act in July. Over three years, the legislation would raise taxation by
around $50 billion and reduce spending by $13 billion. Although the
measure represented his commitment—outlined in the 1984 State of the
Union—to agree a 'down payment' on bipartisan efforts to reduce the
deficit, Reagan was reluctant to alienate conservatives in an election year.
There was no usual ceremony to mark the occasion.[26]

The agreement with China, action on the deficit, and speech about
Vietnam were examples of the Reagan campaign's strategy to fully utilise
the media to maximise not just the president's chances of re-election,
but also the scale of his victory. While the Democrats debated in their
primary contest, the Republicans would emphasise Reagan's 'reality of
strong, confident, successful leadership'. Under this umbrella theme of
leadership, Reagan would also be presented as being competent and
compassionate, combining a belief in 'traditional values' with an optimistic vision of the future. Reagan's campaign was designed to have a

tone of optimism in Reagan's leadership and renewed optimism of Americans in themselves and each other. This emphasis on leadership was timed to coincide with Reagan's European tour, including the G7 Summit and Normandy events, taking advantage of extensive media coverage of Reagan representing the country as president, while the Democrats remained divided.[27] Reflecting Reagan's optimism, the *New York Times* reported that the power of the presidency had been revitalised and that Reagan had 'significantly increased controls to protect the security of his decision-making apparatus, reversing a trend toward more openness under President Carter'.[28] In September 1984, writing a few months before the general election, journalist Hugh Sidey wrote that, 'He has fought bloody diplomatic and legislative battles for nearly four years, and has been excoriated by the Democrats from dawn to dark for the past month, yet the polls show he is liked more than ever by Americans. Why?'[29] His eventual opponent, Mondale, would target the claim that Reagan was competent during the presidential debates in October 1984.

Once Reagan had won the 1984 election, Hugh Sidey would write on the eve of Reagan's second inaugural that, 'The idea that the job was too big for one person has little currency now. The notion, so popular only a few years ago, that one man could not make a difference has been pushed aside…We enter these next four years with the knowledge that the presidency works'.[30] Reagan's character and goals may have been an enigma to many, but what was clear was that he shaped the presidency—as an institution—in accordance with his character and goals which has been seen to have lasting effect. For example, Reagan's executive branch appointments were part of a broader concerted effort to reassert the president's dominance over the executive branch and to safeguard it from legislative oversight.[31] In this light, towards the end of the Reagan administration, some scholars began to speak of his presidency as being 'post-modern' in the sense that Reagan had truly consolidated the expansive changes made to the institution by presidents since Franklin Roosevelt who consolidated the creation of the modern presidency.[32] Though such theses are problematic in the sense they do not truly outline the definitive characteristics of this supposed next stage in the presidency's historical development, they nevertheless convey an academic recognition that Reagan had made considerable institutional changes and set the presidency on a new path from its degenerative state as expressed by its condition throughout the 1970s. For example, presidential scholar Stephen Skowronek's 'regime theory' of the presidency, which produces

30   J. COOPER ET AL.

four types of presidential leadership, considers Reagan as a reconstructive president.[33] The reconstructive president

> found new ways to order the politics of the republic and release the power of government; but they have done so by building personal parties and shattering the politics of the past, actions the Constitution was originally supposed to guard against. Moreover, each of these great political leaders — Jefferson, Jackson, Lincoln, Franklin Roosevelt and Reagan — passed on a newly circumscribed regime, so tenacious as to implicate their successors in another cycle of gradually accelerating political decay.[34]

It is for this reason that that Donald Trump was viewed to have represented 'the final collapse of Reagan-era conservatism'.[35] In fact, Donald Trump's slogan Make America Great Again, which he is also branding for his 2024 campaign, was first invoked by Ronald Reagan during the latter's Republican nomination acceptance speech. Reagan's legacy on the presidency as an institution, the Republican Party, and American politics writ large, is still being felt in contemporary times. The year 1984 signified the culmination of the themes and trends, which solidified Reagan's legacy in this regard. Reagan's reassertion of the presidency was a key aspect of his first term and part of his record for voters to judge in the general election.

Executive Order 12333—Reagan's intelligence activities directive issued in December 1981—altered Jimmy Carter's executive order on intelligence activities by changing a section formerly titled as 'Restrictions on Intelligence Activities' to 'Conduct of Intelligence Activities'.[36] This was a clear attempt at making constraints on executive authority in foreign policy the exception rather than the rule. Reagan, in fact, gave more freedom to his newly appointed CIA director, William Casey (who served in this role 1981–1987), from even White House oversight and accountability although the director was to act, as mandated by Executive Order 12333, 'as the primary adviser to the President and the NSC on national foreign intelligence'.[37] The significance of Executive Order 12333 is also particularly acute as it pertains to the wider historical development, and aggrandisement, of the presidency, which continued after Reagan but was largely made possible because of Reagan.[38] News about the abuses of the National Security Agency (NSA), during the War on Terror era, has often focused on the 2001 USA Patriot Act and blamed this act, signed by George W. Bush, for allowing sweeping abuses and claims of executive power—by intelligence agencies—in fighting terrorism. However,

1984   31

the powers employed during the War on Terror by intelligence agencies, such as the NSA, were done so much more broadly but that these powers actually derive from Reagan's Executive Order 12333.[39] This is because Executive Order 12333 had the full force of law and authorised the National Security Agency to collect the telephone records of millions of Americans and because this order was not a statute and was never put to a congressional vote or undergone a judicial review. Further still, by 1983, it was recognised that the CIA was 'on the rebound'.[40] It is no coincidence that those covert operations of the 1980s that were being sanctioned by the reinvigorated intelligence agency, in Central America, Africa, and Asia, have been referred to as the *Reagan Doctrine Wars* and the *Secret Wars of the CIA, 1981–1987*.[41] One of the CIA's most infamous secret wars, during the Reagan era, was the funding of the Contra rebels in Nicaragua who were attempting to topple the leftist Sandinista government that had taken power in 1979. This policy would morph into the Iran-Contra scandal. However, the roots of this scandal, as it pertained to the policy options and the mechanisms of power employed to execute it, orientate around the year 1984.

Thanks to the re-empowerment of the CIA and the executive branch writ large, as expressed by such aforementioned executive orders, in the first months of 1984, and with presidential approval, the CIA began mining three Nicaraguan harbours.[42] However, after this became public in mid-1984, Congress passed the second Boland Amendment that made it illegal for any government agency—whether it was indirectly or directly—to support the Contras in Nicaragua.[43] The first Boland Amendment of 1982 had already restricted American spending in Nicaragua with the legislation mandating that,

> None of the funds provided in this Act may be used by the Central Intelligence Agency or the Department of Defense to furnish military equipment, military training or advice, or other support for military activities, to any group or individual, not part of a country's armed forces, for the purposes of overthrowing the Government of Nicaragua.[44]

In turn, the Reagan White House would disregard these congressional provisions, and violated them by directing illegally sourced funds, made from Iran and directed them to controversial groups in Latin America, with the attempt of overthrowing socialist governments.[45]

The Reagan administration remained adamant about supporting anti-communist forces in this region and especially in Nicaragua. A 1983 *New York Times* article reported that many members of Congress were angered by the administration's failure to notify them of plans for increased military and intelligence activity in Central America.[46] The Iran-Contra scandal continued to develop when, early in 1984, Washington declared Iran to be a sponsor of terrorism and, therefore, the sending of arms to Iran as barter for hostages' lives contradicted the administration's policy, but also broke U.S. law.[47] Although the nature of the Iran-Contra scandal has a much wider timescale, the key point for this study is that 1984 saw the passage of the second Boland Amendment and the pronouncement of Iran as a state-sponsor of terrorism, which the Reagan administration would secretly ignore, and contradict, in embarking upon the Iran-Contra policy.[48] At a meeting of the National Security Planning Group on 25 June 1984, senior administration figures—including Reagan, Vice President George H. Bush (1981–1989), George Shultz (U.S. secretary of state, 1982–1989), and Caspar Weinberger (U.S. secretary of defence, 1981–1987)—discussed how support for the Contras could continue despite opposition on Capitol Hill, specifically by asking third-party countries to fund the Contra's campaign, therefore bypassing the limitations of the Boland Amendments.[49] There was even a debate about the legality of such action, particularly with regard to it potentially leading to impeachment for the president, between Bush and Baker (who after serving in the Reagan administration would serve as Bush's U.S. secretary of state, 1989–1992), with the latter far more cautious. The discussion closed with McFarlane suggesting that 'none of this discussion … be made public in any way'. Perhaps in an attempt to lighten the mood, Reagan added: 'If such a story gets out, we'll all be hanging by our thumbs in front of the White House'.[50]

1984 was also a year when serious objective analyses of Reagan's reassertion of presidential unilateralism began to arise. Throughout this year, scholars and analysts began to talk about how Reagan had renewed another aspect of presidential power which Arthur Schlesinger, during the 1970s, once said had been a defining characteristic of the *Imperial Presidency*: the war power. In 1984, the Heritage Foundation—a conservative think tank that influenced the Reagan administration's economic policy—published their *Mandate for Leadership II* report in which Stuart Butler praised Reagan's use of military force to halt Soviet expansion in Grenada.[51] Reagan's authorisation to invade Grenada, in October 1983, was the first and only instance when Reagan used military force to remove a Marxist regime from power; he did so without a U.N. resolution and without congressional authorisation. Within a draft speech that Reagan was preparing, Reagan writes—as early as 1980—that, 'Totalitarian Marxists are in control of the Caribbean island of Grenada where Cuban advisors are now training guerrillas for subversive action against other countries'.[52] It is clear that Reagan saw the 1979 Grenadian Marxist revolution as a geostrategic threat in the Cold War and therefore necessary to address. The Reagan Doctrine implied that governments that have come to power without fulfilling the requirements of a democratic process are to be regarded as illegitimate. Consequently, against such illegitimate governments, especially if they were Marxist-Leninist, intervention was justified.[53] However, the invasion, which was codenamed *Operation Urgent Fury*, was legally justified, by the administration, on three main grounds that were outlined by legal adviser, Davis Robinson, to the American Bar Association on 10 February 1984.[54] Those grounds were that: the action was requested by Grenada's Governor-General; the action was part of a legitimate regional collective security initiative permitted by the Organisation of Eastern Caribbean States (OECS); and the action was undertaken to protect American citizens that were potentially in danger in Grenada.[55] Despite the administration's claims that the OECS had requested the administration to intervene militarily to resolve the crisis, the Caribbean leaders had actually voted to suspend Grenada from regional trade agreements, yet not agreed on any particular intervention.[56] On the other hand, the Reagan administration took a public relations blow, in 1983, after the bombing in Lebanon which killed nearly 250 American service personnel, and invading Grenada—knowingly an easy target—served to restore face to the administration.[57] It was during the year 1984 that scholars began to speculate on the implications of this event for the institution of the presidency. One scholar wrote that the Reagan administration utilised the Grenada invasion and successful removal of a Marxist regime as the curing of the Vietnam syndrome; the latter supposedly referring to an American apprehension to get involved militarily because of the experiences of Vietnam.[58] A legal academic, writing in a 1984 edition of the *Virginia Law Review*, in response to Reagan's employment of presidential unilateralism in his authorisation to use force in Grenada, and Lebanon, wrote that,

Anyone wishing to argue that the War Powers Resolution of 1973 is unconstitutional must be prepared to explain the purpose of article I, section 8, clause 11, of the Constitution. That pro- vision expressly grants to Congress the power "To declare War." 2 If the President of the United States is free to fight a war whether or not one has been declared, then this apparently unambiguous constitutional provision is devoid of significance.[59]

It was clear in 1984 that presidential power was once again being overextended.

President Reagan and Vice President Bush at a welcoming rally at the Loews Anatoly hotel in Dallas, Texas (22 August 1984) *Courtesy*: Ronald Reagan Library

President Reagan, Nancy Reagan with George Bush and Barbara Bush during celebration at the Republican National Convention at the Dallas Convention Center, Texas (23 August 1984) *Courtesy*: Ronald Reagan Library

President Reagan, Nancy Reagan, Vice President Bush and Mrs. Bush at the Republican National Convention, Dallas, Texas (23 August 1984) *Courtesy*: Ronald Reagan Library

President Reagan at a Reagan-Bush Rally in Hammonton , New Jersey (19 September 1984) *Courtesy*: Ronald Reagan Library

President Reagan and Democratic candidate Walter Mondale during the second debate on foreign policy in Kansas City, Missouri (21 October 1984) *Courtesy*: Ronald Reagan Library

CAMPAIGNING ABROAD

1984 was a crucial year for the president's prestige on the international stage. Reagan visited three significant arenas as it pertained to the geopolitics of the 1980s: Ireland, China, and continental Europe—the latter as part of the fortieth anniversary of the D-Day invasion. Reagan recalled in his memoir his impressions of the China visit.[60] He noted how the Chinese were coming to accept free markets and inviting investment by foreign capitalists.[61] One particular passage emphasised the fact that, despite the increasing Chinese opening up, there were still tensions being defined by America's Cold War opposition to communist regimes when Reagan recorded that,

> I addressed a group of Chinese civic leaders; a recording of my speech was subsequently broadcast to the Chinese people—minus several of my lines about the Soviet Union, religion, and the value of a free economy. Then came another meeting with Zhao and several party leaders, where we discussed trade and investment. At this meeting, a small, feisty ideologue tried to lecture me about removing our troops from South Korea. I tried to give it right back to him. If North Korea really wanted to improve relations with us, as he claimed it did, let them stop digging illegal tunnels under the demilitarized buffer zone between the two Koreas, I said.[62]

Reagan returned home, heartened by "'the injection of a free market spirit'" into China's economy and optimistic about the prospect for friendship and economic cooperation "with this so-called Communist China'".[63] He welcomed China's opening up to American investment and its non-expansionism. The significance of China must be viewed within the context of the Cold War. In 1986, within an internal discussion between Reagan and his top foreign policy advisers, there is indication that with the arrival of Mikhail Gorbachev on the scene and his dedication to reform and opening up the Soviet Union and its economy, the Reagan administration began to see the Soviet Union as potentially being the next China. George Shultz wrote to Reagan that, 'The China of your Administration could be USSR. Different than detente. Detente was making existing systems interact. Gorb. changing theirs; we interact w/changed system. An aspect of the Reagan doctrine'.[64] Therefore, 1984 can once again centralised in the history of not only the Reagan administration's diplomacy with the People's Republic, but also within the wider relations between the United States and China. Upon his return to the United States, in early May 1984, Reagan told reporters that,

> We went to China to advance the prospects for stability and peace throughout the world. And we went to illustrate, by our presence, our sincere desire for good relations. We went to meet again with the Chinese and review our concerns and our differences. And we went to China to further define our own two countries' relationship -- and, by defining it, advance it.[65]

Despite Reagan's 1984 visit signalling the continuing good relations between the two countries, suspicions remained. For instance, the Defense Intelligence Agency in April 1984 sanctioned a Defense Estimative Brief that conveyed how the Chinese were making qualitative improvements in its nuclear arsenal: 'The Chinese will not try to match the superpowers. The Chinese, however, will continue to seek Western technology support for their underground nuclear test program'.[66] 1984 foreshadowed contemporary tensions.

Commenting on the interplay between Reagan's Chinese trip, the upcoming election, and Reagan's statesmanship, an article in the *New York Times* read that, 'The image of Ronald Reagan, the international statesman, will contrast nicely with news coverage of Walter F. Mondale and Gary Hart moiling and quarrelling in petty grabs for Democratic delegates…With Mr. Reagan's luck, the sun will shine all the time he's in Peking and there won't be a single dust storm'.[67] In contrast, Reagan's visit to Ireland, between 2 and 5 June 1984 was met with widespread protest.[68] Indeed, the visit to Ireland highlighted how small nations played important roles within the history of the Cold War and that the tensions over Reagan's presence in Ireland were an example of the epoch being more complex that the rivalry between to the two superpowers.[69]

Reagan's campaign utilised an extension of the 'rose garden' approach to political campaigns.[70] The president's summer tour of Europe enabled to take advantage of all of the advantages of incumbency, ensuring that he was able to project concurrent messages about both the future and past American successes. In June 1984, the Reagan campaign took full opportunity to gather footage of the president visiting his ancestral roots in Ireland, meeting other world leaders at the G7 summit, and commemorating the fortieth anniversary of D-Day. But the campaign's messages were central to all of these activities. Even in Ireland, among the photo-opportunities of Reagan returning to his ancestral home in Tipperary, the president's peaceful message in the Cold War dominated. In a lengthy speech, mostly about the importance of freedom around the world, delivered at the Irish Parliament (the Dáil Éireann), Reagan explained his position:

> The Soviets seek to place the blame on the Americans for this self-imposed isolation. But they have not taken these steps by our choice. We remain ready for them to join with us and the rest of the world community to build a more peaceful world. In solidarity with our allies, confident of our strength, we threaten no nation. Peace and prosperity are in the Soviet interest as well as in ours. So, let us move forward.[71]

When Reagan was in France for the D-Day commemorations, he declared 6 June to be a 'day of national honour'. In the meantime, the Democrats remained in electoral purgatory, without a clear nominee for the presidential election. Mondale continued to battle Senator Gary Hart (D-CO) to emerge as the standard bearer to take on Reagan. One political advertisement showed Reagan addressing veterans at the D-Day events, where he called them the 'products of the freest society in history'.[72] With his domestic audience in mind, Reagan used the D-Day speeches to continue to emphasise his softer Cold War rhetoric, with him again calling for peace, and even the elimination of nuclear weapons:

It's fitting to remember here the great losses also suffered by the Russian people during World War II: 20 million perished, a terrible price that testifies to all the world the necessity of ending war. I tell you from my heart that we in the United States do not want war. We want to wipe from the face of the Earth the terrible weapons that man now has in his hands. And I tell you, we are ready to seize that beachhead. We look for some sign from the Soviet Union that they are willing to move forward, that they share our desire and love for peace, and that they will give up the ways of conquest. There must be a changing there that will allow us to turn our hope into action.[73]

Reagan also used the opportunity to show his support for allies and articulate the values that untied them:

From a terrible war we learned that unity made us invincible; now, in peace, that same unity makes us secure. We sought to bring all freedom-loving nations together in a community dedicated to the defense and preservation of our sacred values. Our alliance, forged in the crucible of war, tempered and shaped by the realities of the postwar world, has succeeded. In Europe, the threat has been contained, the peace has been kept.[74]

Shortly after returning to the United States, Reagan received a memorandum from McFarlane and Shultz.[75] The president's leading foreign policy figures were concerned that, without wishing to pre-empt his re-election, it was time for them to plan for Reagan's second term, partially as a means to 'expand the Reagan legacy', given that he would enjoy a 'kind of freedom of action' that no re-elected president had done so since Eisenhower (or newly elected one since Kennedy). 1984 therefore represented a moment to 'review first-term accomplishments, assess where we stand now, and have operational strategies ready' for the second term beginning in January. Reagan's legacy could be both consolidated and strengthened by careful planning during the election campaign.[76]

By the end of June, Reagan's job approval was 54%.[77] With Reagan reaping the electoral advantages of association with the United States' 'greatest generation', Thatcher sought to mitigate the difficult politics that the U.S. deficit meant Reagan had to navigate at home, but also abroad when meet meeting other world leaders. The British prime minister hosted the G7 summit and made sure that it would not raise any concerns about the U.S. economy that could be used by Reagan's political opponents.[78] The campaign's interests were at the heart of preparations for Reagan's European visit.[79] Reagan was briefed: 'The settings for the visits are both dramatic and colourful. The return home to Ireland, the lessons and sacrifices associated with Normandy, and the historical stability of London provide an ideal backdrop for your central themes of peace, prosperity, and Alliance solidarity'.[80]

According to *The Washington Post*, the White House expected Reaganomics to be the focus of criticism at the G7.[81] Anglo-American relations turned to the politics of the day, with the British embassy in Washington, D.C. informed London that the Reagan administration sought 'an outcome that will play well in his election campaign'.[82] It was recognised that Reagan wanted to appear 'presidential' and be praised for the 'domestic policy objectives which the President (and indeed most of his summit partners) has been pursuing have paid off in terms of economic recovery'. For instance, on the U.S. deficit, the White House hoped that the G7 would address this in as 'low-key a manner as possible' and indeed had already expressed their thanks for 'the efforts of the President's British hosts have been making to achieve this'.[83] Reagan got his wish. The G7's final communique mentioned deficits once, and this was halfway through, and made no reference to the United States. The G7 called for policies that would reduce inflation, interest rates, and deficits and create more jobs. This mirrored Reagan's campaign messages.[84] Upon the president's return to the United States, the British embassy reported to London:

> Coverage of the entire Reagan European tour in the US media has been massive. The exercise has been presented as a considerable success for the President, with many commentators pointing to the contrast between his performance, speaking for America, and the continuing feuding in the Democrat camp. He is seen as, "acting presidential": the Democrats as "playing politics."[85]

Reagan's international diplomacy was intertwined with certain key events and themes that convalesced and came to the forefront during these trips. The 1984 Los Angeles Olympics also contributed to these themes and Reagan's shift in Cold War policy. Likewise, the Soviets Union's decision to boycott the games perhaps, in hindsight, can be seen as one of the final symbolic gestures of the Cold War. When asked about the boycott, Reagan remarked:

I'm sorry that they feel that way, and I think it's unfair to the young people that have been waiting for so long to participate in those games.

And it ought to be remembered by all of us that the games more than 2,000 years ago started as a means of bringing peace between the Greek city-states. And in those days, even if a war was going on, when Olympic year came, they called off the war in order to hold the games. I wish we were still as civilized.[86]

Welcoming the Olympic torch to Washington, D.C., the president emphasised the connection between the Olympics and peace between competing nations:

The Olympics were started more than 2,000 years ago to hopefully offer a substitute to the constant warfare between the city-states of Greece. They were revived on an international basis nearly a century ago, and again, the goal was peace and understanding. Let us keep that Olympic tradition alive in Los Angeles and resolve that the Olympic flame will burn ever brighter.[87]

No opportunity could be missed in emphasising the president's concern for the future of America's young people or his desire for a thawing in relation with the Soviet Union. When congratulating American athletes after the games had closed, Reagan noted how 'The only losers of the 23d Olympiad were those who didn't or couldn't come'.[88] Yet the politicking did not end with a criticism of the Soviet Union. The president praised athletes from around the world, with particular nods to 'the South Korean boxers, the Chinese gymnasts, the Romanian athletes, the Jamaicans, the Japanese'. Further seeking to soften his own image for the campaign, he was keen to celebrate the diversity of American Olympians: 'And so, I say to you, the great melting pot team of 1984, the members of America's team at the 23d Olympics, thanks for the memories and thanks for the great moments and thanks for being what you are, genuine heroes'. Of course, Reagan did also have to connect American sporting success to his own looming electoral contest: '1984 has a kind of special significance for me … I'm finding it to be a very interesting year'.[89]

1984   43

Election Campaign Ads

The failure of the midterm's slogan that Americans should 'stay the course', coupled with Nancy Reagan's dissatisfaction with the 1980 Reagan campaign advertisements, led to the White House engaging some of the leading advertisers in the United States. Grouped together as the 'Tuesday Team', in a suite above Radio City Music Hall, figures such as Phil Dusenberry from BBDO (who had produced the Michael Jackson advertisements for Pepsi) developed Reagan's campaign commercials. Hal Riney (who worked for Ogilvy and Mather) wanted to focus on emotion instead of a series of negative political advertisements. This task was potentially difficult given Reagan's approval ratings in 1983 and their solid, but not spectacular, figures in 1984. Likewise, unemployment remained higher in 1984 than it had in 1980, and the deficit was a cause of concern. Nonetheless, the Tuesday Team crafted advertisements that showed less of a still potentially divisive president and more a combination of optimism, nostalgia, and message that the country was finally heading in the right direction.[90] Riney wrote much of the key ad copy, while another ad, composed by New York agency's Tom Messner, was an eighteen-minute biographical campaign video for the Republican National Convention in Dallas and was helmed by Dusenberry. The latter was incidentally co-screenwriter for Robert Redford's nostalgic movie *The Natural* that opened that year, summarised by *Variety* as a: 'quite strange, fable about success and failure in America'.[91] This was reflected in the Reagan campaign's desire to compare the president to the failed past under the Carter-Mondale administration: the strategy was to form Reagan into the embodiment of an idealised America.[92] When Reagan spoke at a rally in September 1984, he was already playing this persona: 'I think there's a new feeling of patriotism in our land, a recognition that by any standard America is a decent and generous place, a force for good in the world. And I don't know about you, but I'm a little tired of hearing people run her down'.[93] This was exactly the rhetoric that would be receptive in the United States still reeling from Vietnam and Watergate.[94]

Reagan was trying to seek re-election but also reaffirm the office of the presidency in 1984. The 1970s ravaged confidence in American institutions. By 1975 New York City had become known as 'Fear City',[95] with scaremongering pamphlets being handed out to the remaining tourists, and a headline in the *New York Daily News* declaring President

Gerald Ford had told the city to 'Drop Dead'.[96] Political office was not regarded as a strong, moral guide as it was perhaps under Franklin Delano Roosevelt, Abraham Lincoln, or George Washington, but more now for the corrupt. The application of an affirmative campaign in 1984 was a natural progression of the fight for belief in the institution itself.

In the media, a number of tracks reverberated with the sense of mistrust in society, of a lack of safety, of self-preservation. The most obvious example was Rockwell's *Somebody's Watching Me*.[97] But there was also Bruce Springsteen's *Dancing in the Dark* from his seventh album, *Born in the USA*.[98] Billy Joel's *Innocent Man* spoke to similar disenchantment.[99] This paranoia was underlined by Run DMC's account of *Hard Times*.[100] Indeed, these tracks spoke to a growing paranoia. However, this was not fear of a threat from abroad, but a threat within the borders: a continuing sense of the 1970s having not yet abated, identity still resting on shaky ground as day-to-day existence is still guarded. These records were sold alongside a number of tracks exploring the idea of control, which was appropriate for the year Orwell's novel was set. Examples include: Cyndi Lauper's *She Bop* and Madonna's *Borderline* (as well as the latter's *Holiday* that was also suggesting a desire to escape).[101] Tina Turner's *What's Love Got To Do With It* was not a song purely about romance, while The Pointer Sisters also alluded to vulnerability.[102] There was a feeling of steam building, of a society already starting to feel a sense of unreasonable expectation, to fit a coat for which one size does not fit all. This was underlined by the GoGos and, of course, Kenny Loggins' title track to the movie *Footloose*.[103] The foundation of the approach to the rebuilding of trust in American institutions was in the context of a president who sought a reduced role for government. However, Reagan would express this in terms of national security—which required a greater level of government spending—and the economy, whereby he sought to empower individuals, business, and entrepreneurs.

In terms of national security, the campaign's message would be loud and clear: a stronger America is a safer America and only Reagan was prepared to do what it took to maintain peace with military might. Opinion polls at the time suggested that as many as 70% favoured a freeze in nuclear armament.[104] However, the message was pushed, and budget was pushed, with huge amounts committed to the defence budget, further deepening the deficit and, for his critics, Reagan was only increasing the risk of the Cold War turning hot. The vast sixteen-minute track *Brother Where You Bound* released in 1984 was part of an album of the same name that engaged with Cold War politics. The anti-authoritarian track opened with not only a reading from *1984* but with political sound bites from radio reports about socialism and military tensions.[105] The lyrics speaks of control, threat, hatred, and mistrust.

The movie *Red Dawn* blasted that message home with a dizzying array of automatic weapons.[106] Helmed by director John Milius—who insisted on being called 'The General' on set,[107] and allegedly signed on for $1.25 million and the gun of his choice[108]—and performed by a cast that had endured tough Green Beret training boot camps, *Red Dawn* played out the 'what if' of a Russian invasion of American soil in an alternate present. One of its most famous moments shows a bumper sticker warning: 'They can have my gun when they pry it from my cold dead fingers', before tilting to the dead American owner of the pick-up that displayed it, as a Russian soldier does precisely that.[109] The Reagans screened it on 7 September 1984 at Camp David.[110] As lead Patrick Swayze reflected: 'Red Dawn scared a lot of people. We take our freedom for granted and we think "Oh, it can't happen to us". Red Dawn kind of just stirred the worldwide pot a little bit and got people thinking. And got people scared'.[111] The *New York Times* review called it 'rabidly inflammatory' and 'so incorrigibly gung-ho' with a 'chilling premise... dissipated by wildly excessive directorial fervor at every turn'.[112] The *Washington Post* lamented its 'preposterous dialogue and weary of the string of explosions that passes for plot'[113] and dismissed it as another in a series of the 'seemingly endless Red Nightmare of John Milius'.[114] It was one of the first movies to receive the new PG-13 rating and held the record for most violent film for a time.[115] Director Milius knew what a political hand grenade the piece had the potential to be:

> I knew one thing that would happen. I knew that Hollywood would condemn me for it, you know, that I would be regarded as a right-wing war monger from then on you know totally uncontrollable, unhousebroken. ... At that time, I mean I was the only person in Hollywood would dare do this movie, you know? Hollywood was very left-wing. There's parts of me that are very left-wing, I mean, get me going about corporate greed and I turn into a Maoist. But I, I have a lot of contradictions. I'm a militarist you know, and an extreme patriot at times you know, so I believe in all of that rugged individualism hogwash.[116]

46   J. COOPER ET AL.

On balance, the film focuses on the sensationalist fascination with teenagers committing acts of violence rather than deeply engaging with any Cold War era issues. However, once the summer blockbuster was released, its alarming premise was part of the public consciousness in all its brutal, full colour, and enormity: a threat made far more tangible. In terms of the 1984 re-election campaign, much of Reagan's Cold Warrior credentials were crystallised into the 30-second campaign ad 'Bear', written by Riney, with his voiceover musing simply wile a bear was shown prowling through the forest:

> There is a bear in the woods.
> For some people, the bear is easy to see. Others don't see it at all.
> Some people say the bear is tame. Others say it's vicious, and dangerous.
> Since no one can really be sure who's right, isn't it smart to be as strong as the bear?
> If there is a bear.
> [A man appears, a rifle on his shoulder. The bear takes a slight step backward.]
> [Title card, white on black: *'President Reagan: Prepared for Peace'*].[117]

A lumbering black bear is ominous enough but its use as symbol of Russia deepens the message and intensifies the threat without need for language.[118] The ad was labelled in the *Washington Post* as a 'unique attempt at commercial by parable'.[119] Without having to chance any specifics, the message of the Soviet threat that only Reagan would stand up to the Soviet Union was laid plain in a few short, memorable seconds. With 'the highest recall score of any of the Reagan ads tested in Reagan-conducted focus groups' that year 'officials found in their focus-group tests involving average viewers that The Bear was an extraordinarily effective way to sell Reagan's peace-through-strength message'.[120]

The Reagan campaign's themes were brought together by the 'Morning in America' advertisements, which first aired while the Democrats were still seeking a nominee. These advertisements were the key plank in Reagan's re-election campaign. One such advertisement—'America's Back'—showed a child cycling, a new family home, images of Reagan, an American flag, and closed with the slogan: 'President Reagan, Leadership that's working'. The narrator told the audience:

> During the past year, thousands of families have moved into new homes that once seemed out of reach. People are buying new cars that once

thought they couldn't afford. Workers are returning to factories that just four years ago were closed ... And America is back with a sense of pride people thought we'd never feel again. Now that our country is turning around, why would we ever turn back?[121]

The theme of contrast between Reagan's brighter future and the Democrat's passed failures was clear. Another advertisement showed images of new cars, a wedding, an old man hoisting an American flag in front of an awe-struck child as a child, and a similar narration:

> It's morning again in America ... Today more men and women will go to work than ever before in our country's history ... With interest rates and inflation down, more people are buying new homes and our new families can have confidence in the future. America today is prouder, and stronger, and better. Why would we want to return to where we were less than four years ago?[122]

In an advertisement that focused on inflation, there was footage of a rusting farm, a closed factory, and people returning to work. Reagan himself narrated:

> This was America in 1980, a nation that wasn't working. Interest rates were at an all time high. Inflation was at its highest in 65 years ... So we rolled up our sleeves and showed that working together there's nothing we can't do – Today interest rates are down. Inflation is down. Americans are working again. And so is America. And we'll carry on unafraid and unashamed and unsurpassed.[123]

An alignment between American cultural issues and crafting the right perception of the current state of the national economy was essential for the incumbent president. The United States was still in a state of economic recovery as 1984 began, with that recovery uneven for different income groups. The Reagan era was overseeing deindustrialisation, particularly in the 'rust belt' states, as the demand for heavy industry declined. The image of the 'Morning in America' advertisements contrasted with others seen by Americans on a day-to-day basis. Detroit (Michigan) was famous for its previously thriving automobile industry. However, one of the biggest grossing movies of 1984 was Eddie Murphy's *Beverly Hills Cop*, following Detroit's Axel Foley as he tracks down a friend's killer in the not so perfect streets of Los Angeles. To a degree, it is a premise

48   J. COOPER ET AL.

predicated upon the contrast between the 'have-not' being smarter than the 'haves', as one reviewer put it: 'the shrewdest, hippest, fastest-talking underdog in a rich man's world ...and he wins at every turn'.[124] The opening is unpolished, seemingly uncensored with the feel of newsreel footage. The opening shows a grey scene, factories straddling a dirty river, the 'Ford' logo prominently displayed on a background tower, over which the words 'Beverly Hills' appear, the music nothing but a ticking, metallic introduction. The screen is then 'branded' with a red, incongruous 'cop' stamp and the saxophone-led main theme begins as we cut to a car production plant. Next, the streets, the initial shot, proclaim 'Nice to have you in Detroit' in playful letters, before we find ourselves among the run-down buildings and scenes of deprivation among the residents as the lyric intones 'the heat is on'—sung by Detroit local Glenn Frey—until we finish on an open truck packed with illegal cigarettes. The opening echoes Murphy's film from the previous year, *Trading Places* (1983), though this showcased rich and poor in Philadelphia, alternating between the two throughout, creating a similar effect, to the sound of Mozart's overture to *The Marriage of Figaro* (1786), itself laden with class implications. The *Beverly Hills Cop* opening sequence is a forceful statement, foregrounding resilience in black culture, which contrasts starkly with the polished predominantly white 'easy' life in Beverly Hills that follows for much of the movie.[125]

When considered in the context of its release year, 1984, the opening sequence to Beverley Hills Cop contrasted with 'Morning in America', as created by Riney (indeed, the advertisement, 'Prouder, Stronger, Better', was commonly remembered by its most famous opening line).[126] The visuals skimmed lazily over children, a couple marrying, families, a paperboy, flag raising, all predominantly white faces and all drenched in pastel hues and soft focus, like a New England summer evening. The language emphasised 'our country' and talked of 'young men and women', as if lowering inflation was Reagan's dowry for the bride. It is mornings and weddings, children and new homes—all images of new beginnings and starting over. It is a place at peace, with the fear outside the door that Springsteen highlights not even a shadow in the perfectly manicured park. The ad is rendered in soft, pastel colours similar to those used in *The Natural*, the Robert Redford baseball film also released that year.[127] Set to the music of sentimental strings, images include a paperboy on his bicycle, a family taking a rolled rug into a house and campers raising an American flag. The subtext is that after twenty years of social tumult, assassinations, riots, scandal, an unpopular war, and gas lines, Reagan had returned tranquility to the United States.[128]

'Morning in America' focused on a simple message: it provided positive images with a quarter of the time devoted to watching a couple marry, and the repeated key phrase implied a huge sense of freshness, new beginnings and possibility without narrowing its message to a specific demographic. This was a stark contrast to the opening of *Beverly Hills Cop*.[129] There are other cultural examples voicing discontent with the current state of the nation. Run DMC's *Hard Times*, from their self-titled debut album released in 1984, speaks of anything but soft focus, promising futures.[130] Perhaps their most memorable track from the album, *It's Like That*, was crammed with discontent at the state of the American economy.[131] There is a sense that America's young people were left feeling stifled by economic recession and a lack of opportunities, while being simultaneously blamed for not working hard enough.

New York punk band *Reagan Youth* chose their name to lambaste the fervour they saw in Reagan's young followers and evoke parallels with the Hitler Youth of the 1930s. Their 1984 EP *Youth Anthems for the New Order* (echoing their namesake) was wall to wall anti-Regan sentiment. They countered Reagan's 'Are you better off than you were 4 years ago?' campaign focus by posing the question (Are You) Happy?, following it with a bitter response about a dire future for regular, ordinary Americans.[132] Moreover, they depict an 'average' American young man who complies as a bleak outlook for the future, as 'Degenerated'.[133] Extending the despair further in another track, there are no prospects for the young in Reagan's America. Moreover, for this particular group any sense of democracy is a fallacy.[134] Despite the smaller circulation of the EP, the vicious and caustic feel of this debut collection from a band that regularly played New York's CBGB venue and used Reagan's name is a notable and acidic counter to the sentimentality of the president's re-election campaign.

Bruce Springsteen had his own comments to make that year, releasing his seminal album, *Born in the USA*.[135] The album was not as patriotic as the title could suggest, with title track an anti-Vietnam statement despite its misappropriation since by American conservatives. There was isolation voiced in 'Dancing in the Dark', which is a most sorrowful track.[136] With pessimism underlined by *Cover Me*. The closing track, *My Hometown*, is a

50   J. COOPER ET AL.

lament for the downhill trajectory of Springsteen's hometown.[137] Springsteen was not sharing the Reagan campaign's mantra that the United States could look 'forward with confidence to the future'.

By the time 'Morning in America' had made its mark on the minds of Americans, statistics did not seem to be perhaps quite so important. What voters were hearing instead, what made it through, were messages like that spoken by Reagan in his speech in New Jersey at the Reagan-Bush rally in September 1984: clear, simplistic even, but always patriotic. The president explained:

> We've come through some tough times, but we've come through them together -- all of us, from every race, every religion, and ethnic background. And we're going forward with values that have never failed us when we lived up to them -- dignity of work, love for family and neighborhood, faith in God, belief in peace through strength, and a commitment to protect the freedom which is our legacy as Americans. All that we've done and all that we mean to do is to make this country freer still. America's future rests in a thousand dreams inside your hearts. It rests in the message of hope in songs of a man so many young Americans admire -- New Jersey's own, Bruce Springsteen. And helping you make those dreams come true is what this job of mine is all about.[138]

It's almost ironic, bearing in mind three of Springsteen's lyrics that year were so bitter, that Reagan name-checked New Jersey's famous son. Springsteen's lyrics were, for many, sang obliviously and followed by the rousing chorus of 'Born in the USA'.

One hugely influential movie of 1984, and the highest grossing, was Harold Ramis' *Ghostbusters*, which the Reagans screened in July at Camp David.[139] Call it a blockbuster, call it a Saturday Night Live spin-off, a comedy, a Sci Fi flick, or even, as one commentator suggests, a 'New York movie', *Ghostbusters* has since been adopted by the conservatives into its top 25 conservative movies of all time, a fact that is initially baffling'.[140] But looking deeper, the premise of academics, thrown from their cosy Columbia roles headlong into entrepreneurship, wildly high-interest loans and cut-throat business competition, before taking on the lumbering public government machine—personified by Walter Peck of the EPA—that ultimately creates a living hell for the city that only the (heroic) independent businessmen can solve, is the ultimate Reaganite escapist fantasy. On first finding themselves outside of academia, Ray Stantz paces and laments to Peter Venkman while he lounges with an open container:

Stantz: Personally I liked the University, they gave us money and facilities, we didn't have to produce anything. You've never been out of college. You don't know what it's like out there. I've worked in the private sector. They expect results.[141]"

Venkman: For whatever reasons, Ray - call it fate, call it luck, call it karma - I believe everything that happens for a reason. I believe that we were destined to get thrown out of this dump.

Stantz: For what purpose?

Venkman: To go into business for ourselves. [offers bottle]

Stantz: [drinks] This ecto-containment system that Spengler and I have in mind is going to require a load of bread to capitalize. Where are we going to get the money?

Venkman: [drinks, smiles] I don't know. I don't know.[142]

As Venkman begins to persuade Ray with 'call it fate', music suddenly rises to meet him in the background, uplifting, rising, long sustained chords echoing his almost sung delivery, creating a stirring speech with little effort, pulling us along with him just as Ray is convinced. The gibes at the unproductive university system serve as a counter to the rousing concept of 'business for ourselves', though all is tempered with the frightening cost of it all, interest rates as high as they are, so much so both Venkman and Stantz need a drink just to contemplate the debt. And it's so high, even Venkman can't come up with a solution on the spot, despite his rousing build up, even if he is—similar to Reagan—'a little short on academic credentials, [but] ...long on confidence, charm and salesmanship'.[143]

In the following scene Ray panics about the loan he's secured against his house 'at 19%? You didn't even bargain with the guy', before colleague Egon Spengler warns 'the interest rate alone for the first five years comes to $95,000'. Venkman declares: 'Everybody has three mortgages these days. ...Will you guys relax? We are on the brink of establishing *the* indispensable defense science of the next decade: professional paranormal investigations and eliminations. The franchise rights alone will make us rich beyond our wildest dreams'.[144] This is not a blue-collar worker looking to take care of their family. This is not a focus on a service. This is the new Reagan-era American dream, speculate to accumulate, not only generate income, but generate more ways of generating income, with limitless potential. It seems fitting that when they first look around the firehouse they take on as their premises it has a large dollar sign scrawled in the filth on the front window.

Though there is much that could be extrapolated from *Ghostbusters* and little space here, the scene with the Mayor at City Hall towards the end of the movie cannot be overlooked. The Mayor himself is knowingly outlined in the screenplay as: 'a likeable Democrat and a man of the people -- particularly the Irish, Italian and Jewish people'.[145] He is fully aware of the voting power of those communities in New York City and lending more impact to the arrival of the Archbishop in the scene—who calls him 'Lenny'—and the talk of 'biblical proportions...fire and brimstone'. When Venkman seizes the opportunity to talk his way to what he wants, he plays directly to the Mayor: 'If I'm wrong nothing happens. We go to jail: peacefully, quietly, we'll enjoy it. But if I'm right? And we can stop this thing? Lenny? You will have saved the lives of millions of registered voters'.[146] The currency of office is at stake.

The Ghostbusters eventually uncover a Gozer cult that made use of the positioning and ziggurat-style upper construction of the Art Deco skyscraper at 55 Central Park West to intensify their worship, and it is not the only instance of 1930s being referenced that year.[147] Several movies looked back to the interwar period during 1984, specifically that key period of trial in America's past: the Great Depression of the 1930s. Supertramp's music video for their single *Better Days* lampooned this nostalgic gazing, featuring footage from the Great Depression and the Wall Street Crash, of poverty and desperation, scenes emphasising the struggle, and featuring Reagan's voice sampled ironically over the ending: 'Our nation is poised... for greatness'.[148] Within the top 25 grossing movies that year, *The Natural* (with Robert Redford, settling in New York City around 1939), *Places in the Heart* (with Jon Malkovich and Sally Field, set in 1935 Waxahachie Texas), Clint Eastwood and Burt Reynolds team-up *City Heat* (set in Kansas City, 1933), and of course Spielberg's *Indiana Jones and the Temple of Doom* (set in 1935)[149] and even a Steve Martin movie (*All of Me*) used Cole Porter's 1931 jazz standard as its title and theme.[150]

Temple of Doom opens with a slew of period references, from Porter's *Anything Goes* (1934, from his musical of the same name, here apparently sung in Chinese[151]). This was a Busby Berkley parody, a Shanghai gangster fight and pistol shoot-out car chase, with characters being inspired by 1930s Saturday matinée serials, pulp magazines and boys' adventure stories. These were the baby boomers' childhood images and memories. It also owes a great deal to the 1939 film *Gunga Din*—starring Cary Grant and Douglas Fairbanks Jr., with its British officers and Thuggee cult working to expel them—as well as the character of Allan Quartermain in films such as King Solomon's Mines (1937), as the Rank Organization reference evokes with the struck gong as the movie opens. *Gunga Din* was even the first film the Reagans screened together at Camp David in 1984.[152] Its initial setting—Shanghai—was also of great American interest in the 1930s, principally for economic reasons, but East Asian culture was also celebrated and appropriated through the art and culture of the era.[153] Hollywood was celebrating the era of Reagan's hero, Franklin Delano Roosevelt, and it was remembering what it was like to believe in a president again. Hollywood was reminding American audiences that it had already survived challenging times and should take pride in its resilience.

The box office of 1984 was brimming with movies that presented hypermasculine leading male characters. Within the top 20 highest grossing movies that year were *The Terminator, Indiana Jones and the Temple of Doom, Romancing the Stone,*[154] *Greystoke: The Legend of Tarzan,*[155] *Red Dawn* and *Beverly Hills Cop* together with the successful, physically focused *The Karate Kid*.[156] America was still reeling from the public emasculation of the Vietnam War: American manhood was no longer the unstoppable juggernaut, the cavalry called in to end the world war. Hollywood's response was actors such as Arnold Schwarzenegger, Sylvester Stallone, and Steven Seagal, and one-word title films like *Rambo* (1986), *Commando* (1985), *First Blood* (1982), *Predator* (1987), and *Rocky* sequels (1982 & 1985). This was pushed even further with the collision of hypermasculine and tech-heavy science fiction in *The Terminator* (1984) and later in *RoboCop* (1987): cyborgs depicting an extreme defeminisation of a protagonist.[157] Among the Hollywood blockbusters that year, the Reagan campaign sought to emphasise spending on defence and a focus on making the American military machine the strongest and most feared in the world. As noted above, the fortieth anniversary of the D-Day landings was capitalised upon as a political opportunity, with Reagan travelling to France to deliver an ardent speech—peppered with references to prayer, God, and the bible—before veterans at the windswept cliffs of Point-du-Hoc on June 6, with some of the simplest lines coming across as the most heartfelt (underlined here for emphasis):

> These are the boys of Pointe du Hoc. These are the men who took the cliffs. These are the champions who helped free a continent. These are the heroes who helped end a war. ...Forty summers have passed since the battle

that you fought here. You were young the day you took these cliffs; some of you were hardly more than boys, with the deepest joys of life before you. Yet, you risked everything here. Why? Why did you do it? What impelled you to put aside the instinct for self-preservation and risk your lives to take these cliffs? What inspired all the men of the armies that met here? We look at you, and somehow we know the answer. It was faith and belief; it was loyalty and love. ...You all knew that some things are worth dying for. One's country is worth dying for, and <u>democracy is worth dying for,</u> <u>because it's the most deeply honorable form of government ever devised by</u> <u>man.</u> All of you loved liberty. All of you were willing to fight tyranny, and you knew the people of your countries were behind you. ...We are bound today by what bound us 40 years ago, the same loyalties, traditions, and beliefs. We're bound by reality. The strength of America's allies is vital to the United States, and the American security guarantee is essential to the continued freedom of Europe's democracies. We were with you then; we are with you now. Your hopes are our hopes, and your destiny is our destiny.[158]

Hyper masculinity in popular culture was not only a response to international events. In domestic terms, American masculinity was in crisis. Michael Moore's documentary *Roger and Me* (1988) would explore the effects of Reaganism in Flint, Michigan, particularly following the closure of the GM plant. For Moore, former blue-collar works were now alienated, struggling to recognise any meaning.[159] On the international stage, American masculinity was fiercely asserting itself, notably through the rapid militarisation of U.S. defence in the Cold War. Yet, at home, deindustrialisation was robbing huge swathes of manual workers of their role in society, stealing their sense of being integral to America's functioning as a country. As real estate salesman Levene bitterly spits out in Mamet's testosterone-drenched 1984 play *Glengarry Glen Ross*: 'A man's his job and you're f**ked at yours'.[160] The belief in the American dream, the pioneer—the western lone gunman, the solo private detective, the man with no name, even the survivalist—all provide Americans with a very clear picture of the independent person: a self-reliant, 'free' American, equating with being a tough and uncompromising man that pulled himself up by his own bootstraps. The pioneer myth sits at the heart of the American Dream, a fantasy rooted in the travelling west in search of gold, of what Indiana Jones described as 'fortune and glory'.[161] These dreams have been paraded before the American people by the movies. As actor Bill Youmans observed:

1984   55

In America, the popular conception of manhood has always come primarily from movies. The male protagonists of the silver screen, from John Wayne to Sean Connery to Harrison Ford to George Clooney to Denzel Washington, have defined our ideal of what a man should be. In movies, men's cleaned-up, choreographed, heroic representations of gunfire and fistfights have presented for us romanticized, highly unrealistic notions of what violence is all about. We have accordingly developed a warped sense of how to handle aggression.[162]

Reagan's previous career in Hollywood meant that he was the perfect candidate to propagate these ideas as an incumbent president seeking re-election in 1984.

Reagan's not inconsiderable screen time—through everything from silver screen lead roles to the General Electric sponsored television theatre episodes he also presented—had created an image of him in many traditional hypermasculine roles: cowboy, secret agent operative, fast-talking bomber pilot, submarine captain, and American football star. Even his nickname, 'the Gipper', originated from his portrayal of Notre Dame College football star George Gipp in the movie *Knute Rockne, All American* (1940). This meant that before he took to the political stage, there had already formed a particularly masculine persona around him in the minds of the public. Indeed, his Secret Service codename was 'Rawhide'. Reagan's 1984 campaign was able to successfully capitalise on what was effectively the president's brand, thereby presenting him as the tough, no-nonsense, all-American hero, straight into a receptive media landscape.

Although Reagan did not see any wartime action on the front lines, there was cinematic footage of him as a war hero. One instance finds him boldly mapping the Sea of Japan, holding out until the very last moment to surface while his vessel's boiler room flooded.[163] We watch his face agonise over tough decisions at the periscope, then leap into the sea when he is forced to abandon the submarine. In another, we watch him 'drop a tonne of TNT on a pin prick' then fast talk his way 'Jersey-style', loaded with double-speak and technobabble, out of giving military secrets away to a German officer, turning it to his advantage and knocking 'Iron Fist' with a 'glass jaw' out in one punch.[164] It may not have been genuine peril, but movie audiences had been right there with him, and Reagan's ability as an actor to believe what he delivered helped to ensure that not only did he keep delivering these roles across the 1940s, 1950s, and 1960s, but that they were still etched in living memory whenever his name was mentioned.

Reagan's tough guy persona was always tempered with a sense of fairness, and, outside of his war roles, his appearances in westerns often showcased this, such as his undercover army operative cowboy Farrell in *Cattle Queen of Montana* (1954) opposite Barbara Stanwyck, who rides through the picture, appearing as an occasional white knight while gathering the evidence to stop the illegal gun supplies to the local Blackfoot Native American tribe.[165] Another example is Marshal Frame Johnson in *Law and Order* (1953), a man who has already 'cleaned up' Tombstone.[166] He moves to Cottonwood to settle down and finds anything but quiet. Johnson warns: 'You wanted law and order in this town, you got it. I'll shoot the first man that starts for those steps" and taunts a threat to "cut [him]... down to size" with 'I'm kinda lookin' forward to it'. The trailer declared: 'Law was his pledge, order was his creed, despite the fury of outlaw hate and renegade guns'. Reagan had clearly found a niche with old school heroes. With this in his arsenal, ads showed 'him on horseback in a cowboy hat, a vital rough-riding rebuke to namby-pamby liberalism', and indeed we do see him riding on his ranch towards the end of the Republican National Convention film.[167] Reagan also starred in a series of films as Lieutenant 'Brass' Bancroft, Secret Service 'Operative 207'.[168] The trailers for which made such claims as 'Join operative 207 again as he sets out on his most dangerous assignment. ...It's thrilling. It's chilling. Based on the actual records of Wm. H. Moran Ex-chief of the US Secret Service'.[169] These films were to have a very direct impact upon his political career. In turn, the re-election campaign was not afraid to capitalise on the 1981 failed assassination attempt. The footage of the incident constituted a segment of the Convention film, demonstrating on the screen Reagan's ability to defy death in even the most dangerous of situations. In a strange irony, the bodyguard that saved Reagan inspired to become part of the Secret Service after watching Reagan as an operative in one of his Brass Bancroft movies.[170] The attempted assassin, John W. Hinckley Jr., had been obsessed with Scorsese's *Taxi Driver* and Jodie Foster's role within it, believing his act would impress the actress. Out of respect for not only a president—but also a fellow actor—the Academy Awards were postponed for 24 hours. Following surgery, Reagan requested a television screen to be placed in his hotel room so he didn't miss the ceremony. When he spoke to Nancy after surgery, he was reported to have apologised with 'Honey, I forgot to duck'. This was the exact same—and famous—line that boxer Jack Dempsey had offered to his wife Estelle after losing his World Heavyweight title in 1926.[171] In fact, Reagan made a habit of collecting inspirational quotations to use in his speeches as well as using lines from movies in everyday life, such as *Dirty Harry*'s 'Go ahead. Make my day', in response to Congress increasing taxes.[172]

THE GENERAL ELECTION

Mondale secured the Democrat's nomination in July 1984, marginally ahead of Senator Gary Hart (D-CO). Taking full advantage of incumbency, the Reagan campaign resolved to utilise issues, timed around presidential events and travel plans, to maximise coverage in the media. Such issues included the economy and Reagan's work to secure lasting peace with the Soviet Union. This strategy saw Reagan visit agricultural and industrial areas in the Midwest when on his way to Texas for the Republican National Convention (RNC). Leadership was to remain the umbrella theme for the campaign, with a determination to ensure that the Democrats were always reacting to the Republicans agenda, with Reagan clear in his accomplishments that all constituencies had benefited from his leadership, but mitigating criticism by not denying that problems remained.[173]

As the question of presidential leadership was a key topic in the election, commentators spoke of how Reagan had renewed confidence in the presidential office from its decay during the 1970s.[174] One journalist wrote that, 'Reagan has clearly stepped into the front ranks of those American Presidents who, since World War II, have been willing to employ military force as an instrument of national policy'.[175] 1984 must, therefore, be seen as a crucial year for the shaping of understandings regarding Reagan's presidential leadership because of how centralised this issue was within the discourse surrounding the national debate on the election. During the second presidential debate, Mondale criticised Reagan's leadership when he suggested that Reagan's supposed ignorance about terrorist acts being committed by insurgent groups financed by the Reagan administration, in Central America, was an example of his lack of control over foreign policy.[176] However, Reagan's first term had consolidated in the minds of many that the operationalisation of the presidency was possible if the incumbent was able to assert his presidential authority to execute a vision. Richard Reeves of the *New York Times* wrote:

After almost four years of strong Reagan leadership, it is clear that the two parties are looking at the country from opposite ideological directions. There is a big difference between seeing a big, clumsy government as protector or as oppressor, as friend or as foe. The difference has not changed the governing of the United States - yet. In the next four years, though, it could be a different place, as it was after Franklin D. Roosevelt.[177]

Reeves continued: 'Reagan has made a mockery of the conventional wisdom that the country was ungovernable. He has proved to be his own man, a strong leader. He put together an Administration capable of effecting real change in the Government – a government whose leader believed that the Government was the nation's principal problem'.[178]

Another *New York Times* article wrote that 'one campaign issue dominates: the leadership of Ronald Reagan'.[179] A *Washington Post* article referenced its national poll which 'showed 72 percent of those surveyed saying Reagan has strong leadership qualities, while 58 percent said Mondale lacks them'.[180] It is clear that Reagan's reassertion of the presidency and his restoration of confidence in the office was a large contributing factor to his success in the 1984 election. In turn, Reagan's electoral success stemmed not necessarily from his policies, which many polls of the time indicated many people disagreed with, but because he was able to assert his authority and sustain his authority for his actions to guide American politics into a new direction.[181]

After a bruising primary campaign, former Vice President Walter Mondale finally accepted the Democrat's nomination for president on 19 July 1984. Attempting to turn the party's divisions into a positive, he name-checked each of his former rivals, and his choice of vice-presidential candidate, at the beginning of his speech:

> Behind us now is the most wide open race in political history.
> It was noisy - but our voices were heard. It was long - but our stamina was tested. It was hot - but the heat was passion, and not anger. It was a roller coaster - but it made me a better candidate, and it will make me a stronger president of the United States ... We're all here tonight in this convention speaking for America. And when we in this hall speak for America, it is America speaking.
> When we speak of family, the voice is Mario Cuomo's.
> When we speak of change, the words are Gary Hart's.
> When we speak of hope, the fire is Jesse Jackson's.

When we speak of caring, the spirit is Ted Kennedy's.
When we speak of patriotism, the strength is John Glenn's.
When we speak of the future, the message is Geraldine Ferraro.
And now we leave San Francisco - together.[182]

Mondale's decision to invite Rep. Geraldine Ferraro (D-NY) to join the ticket as the first female nominee for vice president was historic and underlined his hope that when he was sworn in for a second term in 1989, he would 'swear to "preserve, protect, and defend" a Constitution that includes the Equal Rights Amendment'. Mondale's political strategy was one that showed his party had listened after the 1980 election:

> We know that America must have a strong defense, and a sober view of the Soviets.
> We know that government must be as well-managed as it is well-meaning.
> We know that a healthy, growing private economy is the key to the future
> ...
> Look at our platform. There are no defense cuts that weaken our security; no business taxes that weaken our economy; no laundry lists that raid our Treasury.
> We are wiser, stronger, and focused on the future. If Mr. Reagan wants to re-run the 1980 campaign: Fine. Let them fight over the past. We're fighting for the American future - and that's why we're going to win this campaign.

In an attempt to portray his party as that with the right vision for the country, Mondale listed charges against Reagan's record:

> One last word to those who voted for Mr. Reagan.
> I know what you were saying. But I also know what you were not saying.
> You did not vote for a $200 billion deficit.
> You did not vote for an arms race.
> You did not vote to turn the heavens into a battleground.
> You did not vote to savage Social Security and Medicare.
> You did not vote to destroy family farming.
> You did not vote to trash the civil rights laws.
> You did not vote to poison the environment.
> You did not vote to assault the poor, the sick, and the disabled.

In a throwback to Reagan's concluding remarks in his 1980 debate with Carter, Mondale summarised: 'Four years ago, many of you voted for Mr.

Reagan because he promised you'd be better off. And today, the rich are better off. But working Americans are worse off, and the middle class is standing on a trap door'.[183]

Of course, the Mondale campaign was fighting an electoral contest that had already been defined by his opponents. One Reagan advertisement took ownership of the term 'Reaganomics' way from its critics of the 1982 midterms, claiming its success was evident compared to the alternative that was on offer to Americans. The advertisement explicitly argued that a Mondale presidency would increase taxation (which he could not deny having admitted this would be a necessity in his convention address). The narration explained:

> With Reaganomics you cut taxes, with Mondalenomics, you raise taxes ... With Reaganomics you cut deficits through growth and less government spending, with Mondalenomics you raise taxes. With Reaganomics you create incentives that will move us forward, with Mondalenomics, you raise taxes. They both work, the difference is Reaganomics works for you, Mondalenomics works against you.[184]

The message was clear: Reagan was for voters' interests while Mondale would make their lives more difficult. As with the previous 'Morning in America' advertisements, the Reagan campaign's themes were those identified by Wirthlin and the Republicans: the campaign to re-elect the president framed the election as a choice between the failed past of Carter and the Democrats, compared to what was presented as brighter future with the president.

The Republican platform at their party convention argued:

> We brought about a new beginning. Americans are better off than they were four years ago, and they're still improving. Almost six and one-half million have found jobs since the recovery began, the largest increase in our history. One and one-half million have come in manufacturing—a part of our economy designated for stagnation and government control by Democrats. More than 107 million Americans, more than ever before, are working. Their industry proves that policies which increase incentives for work, saving, and investment do lead to economic growth, while the redistributionist policies of the past did cause unemployment, declining incomes, and idle industries.[185]

As planned, the message sought to mitigate any concerns or questions that voters had about Reagan's compassion and care about issues of unemployment and inequality: 'We must help the poor escape poverty by building an economy which creates more jobs, the greatest poverty fighter of them all. Not to help the poor is to abandon them and demean our society; but to help the poor without offering them a chance to escape poverty is ultimately to degrade us all'.[186] Billy Joel's *Uptown Girl* played into the concept that 'Prouder, Stronger, Better' was selling, blending worlds like *Trading Places* (1983) and *Beverly Hills Cop* (1984). The lyrics were a collision of high and low, the haves and have-nots.[187] The music video depicted an 'Uptown Cosmetics' model—and Joel's future wife—climbing from a Rolls Royce before a group of auto-mechanics before leaving with one on a motorcycle, the sound harking back to Frankie Valli tracks of the 1960s.[188] The result would not look out of place as a scene from 1970s musical *Grease*.[189] This belief in a hope for the 'average Joe' seemed to be seeping into the consciousness of the country. In the film prepared for the RNC, one of the vox pop interviewees—a blue-collar worker in his thirties—proudly stated in his Eastern European accent: 'He put me to work, he's gonna keep me there. The man did a good job and I hope he's gonna go for another four years. God Bless America'. Another male interviewee (white, aged in his sixties or seventies): 'We're on the upward swing and the factories are working much stronger than before. The people are getting back to work'. A third (male) interviewee (Italian-American accent): 'The economy has never been as great as it has been now in 20 years. Unemployment is down, interest rates are down, more people are buying homes than ever before... We're back on top'.[190] Given the emphasis on hard work in this film, there's something almost poetic about the fact that 'Prouder, Stronger, Better' was, by Rainey's account, written along with all his other ads in a San Francisco bar under the heavy influence of bourbon.[191]

Some attention has been given to Reagan's *see-pause-say* technique for the presentation of prepared speeches.[192] This was particularly prominent in key set-piece events such as campaign speeches. Ken Khachigian, former speechwriter for the president, recalled: 'He explained to me that he did that on purpose...[t]hat was what he called a stage pause, and it was an attention getter'.[193] Reagan was a trained performer; listening to him present from a teleprompter, it is clear he has the breath control to deliver long and complex lines without pausing for breath. When he speaks to camera in longer pieces and aims

62   J. COOPER ET AL.

for genuine connection with his audience, his pauses for emphasis—not for breathing control—are masterfully used. These pauses echo many of those speeches in the movies of the 1940s. Bacall uses them as Vivian when her character first meets Marlowe in *The Big Sleep* (1946). There are many instances in films from this era—Cary Grant, Jimmy Stuart, Humphrey Bogart, Dana Andrews, Fred MacMurray—and indeed it seems to have been either a quirk that got picked up by a number of actors or something explicitly taught through the studio system. They are most commonly at moments of tension or emotion. The most frequent use by far comes from Bing Crosby—an actor it must be noted, Reagan especially admired.[194] This use of pause by Crosby carries a sense of the genuine, honest emotion. This effect was clearly not lost on Reagan, with the convention's eighteen-minute film about him as a case in point. During the section where he discusses the military in Korea, his pauses (denoted with a circumflex '^') here fall thus: 'I hope that people out there recognize what a ^ wonderful bunch of young people we've got in the military now. When they see someone in the street in uniform I ^ hope they'll go up and say hello and ^ maybe tell them they're a little proud'. Again, discussing the assassination attempt, Reagan recalled:

And the next thing I knew, Jerry'd - Secret Service - had simply grabbed me here and threw me ^ into the car, and then he dived in on top of me. ...And it was only then that I felt a paralyzing pain. And I'd learned that the bullet hit me ^ up here.
[cut to mid-shot Reagan in plaid shirt:]
When I walked in they were just concluding ^ a meeting in the hospital of all the doctors ...
[Intercut photo of Reagan smiling opposite Cardinal Cooke at the White House, zoom in on Cooke]
I've been asked to- about a visitor that I had while I was recuperating back in ^ March of 1981, ^ Cardinal Cooke. He was a wonderful man. A most dedicated man, and ^
[resume Reagan in plaid mid-shot, talking direct to camera. Music: soaring strings]
just one of the most kindly men ^ that I have ever met. And we were talking about some of the- ^ call them coincidences, that had happened at the time of the ^ shooting, and that I had heard ^ after ^ I'd started to recover. And he said that ^ in view of them ^ God must have been sitting

on my shoulder. Well ^ he must have been. I told him ^ whatever time I've got left, ^ it now belongs to [points upwards] ^ someone else.
[Fade to black as Reagan looks down.][195]

The effect is mesmerising when combined with the use of close ups, soft focus and footage of troops of the assassination, newspaper headlines, and judiciously chosen sentimental music at these points. There is a real sense that for the viewer that they are sitting in with someone who is being honest with them personally, confiding in them at these moments. And once the viewer notices it, it cannot be missed. For the closing speech in the same video:

[Music starts to 'shimmer' as we pan around personal photographs and furniture in the Oval Office:]
Sitting the Oval Office, you look around and ^ sometimes you can't help but ^ choke up a little bit because you're surrounded by ^ history that somehow has ^ touched everything in this room. And it occurs to you that every person, who ever sat here he earned in the depths of his soul, to bring people and ^ nations together in peace.
Four times in my life America's been at war. That's a tragic ^ waste of ^ lives. And it makes you realize how desperately ^ the world needs a lasting peace. Just across the hall here in the White House of the Roosevelt Room, named after the two Roosevelts who served here: one a Republican, one a Democrat. Many decisions are made in that room, and often as I ^ meet with my staff I gaze up at the ^ 5 service flags, each representing one of the five military services. And draped from each flag are ^ battle streamers signifying every battle campaign fought since the Revolutionary War. Each ribbon a remembrance of a time when American men and women, spilled their blood into the soil of distant lands.
[Camera pulls back to mid-shot as Reagan holds a pen at the Oval Office desk.]
My fondest hope for this presidency, is that the people of America, give us the continued opportunity, to pursue a peace so strong and so lasting, that we'd never again ^ have to add another streamer ^ to those flags.[196]

This conversational connection with the viewer foregrounds a woman who is then shown to be effusing about the president: 'I think he's just doggone honest, it's remarkable. He's been on television-What have I heard? 26 times? Talking to us about what he's doing? Now that's... He's not doing that for any other reason than to make it real clear. And if anybody has any question about where he's headed it's their fault. Maybe they don't have a television'.[197] It is almost as if Reagan exists on the screen, as if that is where he can always be found, as if the two have become indivisible in the public consciousness. The great communicator was always there to explain, reassure, and make the case for America.

Before the convention video ends, Reagan is shown spending time on his ranch, riding horses, and chopping wood. The images and the language chosen are even more 'homely', even more simplified than at any other point in the piece. This is one last clear attempt to establish Reagan as ordinary citizen. The sense of 'aw shucks' honesty is underlined with the choices such as 'o'God's' and 'felt like a quitter', as if pulled from the pages of a 1930s movie screenplay, the pauses once again lending a feel of spontaneity, despite the scripting:

> Before I ^ reached my decision to run for re-election, some people thought that maybe I'd be happy to retire to that beautiful ranch outside Santa Barbara and ^ spend the rest of my life enjoying the simple things: riding horses chopping wood and spending time with Nancy. Being outdoors and close to all o'God's natural gifts.
> But they forget. There are so many things that ^ remain to be done. So many challenges that must be met.
> *[Crossfade to Reagan seated in Oval Office, CU, customary black suit of authority:]*
> I'd have felt like a quitter if ^ I just walked away from getting federal spending under control once and for all. Or from reforming and simplifying our tax system, or ^ creating Enterprise Zones, a set of incentives that would encourage business to ^ help rebuild the troubled areas of our country. Provide hope to those who yearn for true opportunity.[198]

In his own speech to the RNC, Reagan returned to one of his most memorable lines in the 1980 debate with Carter: 'In 1980 we asked the people of America, 'Are you better off than you were 4 years ago?' Well, the people answered then by choosing us to bring about a change. We have every reason now, 4 years later, to ask that same question again, for we have made a change'.[199] Reagan was again pointing to his achievements and an optimistic view of the future. In 1936, Franklin Roosevelt mocked the Republicans for claiming that they would also deliver his economic programme but at a lower cost.[200] Forty-eight years later, the Democrats were the subjects of Republican laughter for suggesting that they could deliver a superior vision to what Reagan was offering. Reagan simply asked voters to remember four years previously and compare it to the present and future he was offering. In his own acceptance speech, the following month, Reagan listed in detail the failings of the Carter years—at home and abroad. The president refused to entertain the notion that the Democrats has listened to the American people in 1980:

> I've been campaigning long enough to know that a political party and its leadership can't change their colors in 4 days. We won't, and no matter how hard they tried, our opponents didn't in San Francisco. We didn't discover our values in a poll taken a week before the convention. And we didn't set a weathervane on top of the Golden Gate Bridge before we started talking about the American family.[201]

He even used the Democrats' own key metrics from the 1970s—the so-called misery index—to emphasise his argument:

> And while we have our friends down memory lane, maybe they'd like to recall a gimmick they designed for their 1976 campaign ... adding the unemployment and inflation rates, they got what they called a misery index. In '76 it came to 12 1/2 percent. They declared the incumbent had no right to seek reelection with that kind of a misery index. Well, 4 years ago, in the 1980 election, they didn't mention the misery index, possibly because it was then over 20 percent. And do you know something? They won't mention it in this election either. It's down to 11.6 and dropping.[202]

These competing accounts of America's past and future collided in two presidential debates in October 1984. The first debate, held on 7 October, focused on domestic issues. It was widely viewed to be a successful evening for Mondale and a disastrous one for Reagan. Mondale's campaign was buoyed by their candidate's performance, believing that Mondale had opened up the contest.[203] The *New York Times* reported that the president 'appeared more subdued and was sometimes tentative in his answers', with his voice 'noticeably quavering, particularly in the early going', and he even 'appeared angry at suggestions that he lacked compassion', which was a sensitive issue for the Reagan campaign.[204] The debate culminated in closing remarks. However, there was some confusion between Reagan and the moderators as to whether he was due a rebuttal to Mondale's final critique of his record (on the topic of deficits) before both candidates concluded the evening. While the mix-up can be attributed to Barbara Walters' handling of the questions, Reagan's admission that he was confused after a lengthy and fierce debate hardly supported his credibility for a second term:

> *Ms. Walters*: Thank you very much. We must stop now. I want to give you time for your closing statements. It's indeed time for that from each of you. We will begin with President Reagan.
>
> Oh, I'm sorry, Mr. Reagan, you had your rebuttal, and I just cut you off because our time is going. You have a chance now for rebuttal before your closing statement. Is that correct?
> *The President*: No, I might as well just go with-
> *Ms. Walters*: Do you want to go with your-
> *The President*: I don't think so. I'm all confused now.
> *Ms Walters*: Technically, you did. I have little voices that come in my ear. [Laughter] You don't get those same voices. I'm not hearing it from here--I'm hearing it from here.
> *The President*: All right.
> *Ms. Walters*: You have waived your rebuttal. You can go with your closing statement.[205]

As was typical in the campaign, both candidates chose to look back to the key moment of the 1980 debate as a means to project their vision for the future. Reagan explained,

> Four years ago, in similar circumstances to this, I asked you, the American people, a question. I asked: "Are you better off than you were 4 years before?" The answer to that obviously was no, and as the result, I was elected to this office and promised a new beginning.
>
> Now, maybe I'm expected to ask that same question again. I'm not going to, because I think that all of you--or not everyone, those people that are in those pockets of poverty and haven't caught up, they couldn't answer the way I would want them to--but I think that most of the people in this country would say, yes, they are better off than they were 4 years ago.
>
> The question, I think, should be enlarged. Is America better off than it was 4 years ago? And I believe the answer to that has to also be "yes." I promised a new beginning. So far, it is only a beginning. If the job were finished, I might have thought twice about seeking reelection for this job.

The president was clearly recognising that serious problems remained but was adamant that his leadership was working. Mondale also utilised this rhetorical device, seeking to condemn Reagan's record in a final flourish that could serve as a microcosm of his overall debate performance:

> Are we better of with this arms race? Will we be better off if we start this star wars escalation into the heavens? Are we better off when we de-emphasize our values in human rights? Are we better off when we load our children with this fantastic debt? Would fathers and mothers feel proud of themselves if they loaded their children with debts like this nation is now--over a trillion dollars on the shoulders of our children? Can we say, really say that we will be better off when we pull away from sort of that basic American instinct of decency and fairness?[206]

Reagan diarised: 'Well the debate took place & I have to say I lost' although Mondale 'kept repeating things that are absolute falsehoods'.[207] Ever the optimist, president was more cheerful after attending a large campaign rally on 8 October, where the thousands in attendance 'had all seen the debate & thought I'd won'.[208]

During the second debate, Reagan was asked directly about his previous debate performance and the questions that it has prompted about his capacity to serve as president. One of the moderators, Henry Trewhitt (*Baltimore Sun*) began an exchange with Reagan which is one of the most recognisable debate moments in the presidential campaigns:

> Mr. President, I want to raise an issue that I think has been lurking out there for 2 or 3 weeks and cast it specifically in national security terms. You already are the oldest President in history. And some of your staff say you were tired after your most recent encounter with Mr. Mondale. I recall yet that President Kennedy had to go for days on end with very little sleep during the Cuban missile crisis. Is there any doubt in your mind that you would be able to function in such circumstances?[209]

Reagan's response prompted laugher throughout the room, even with Mondale: 'Not at all, Mr. Trewhitt, and I want you to know that also I will not make age an issue of this campaign. I am not going to exploit, for political purposes, my opponent's youth and inexperience'.[210] Reviewing the debate, the conservative *National Review* observed that Reagan had successfully reassured voters of eloquence and stance on key issues.[211] Nonetheless, it was in the same debate that Reagan misspoke about events that would lead to the Iran-Contra scandal. Commenting on the issue of covert American action in Nicaragua in support of the Contras' efforts to overthrow the Marxist Sandinista regime, as it emerged through the finding of a CIA manual, the president revealed too much detail:

> I have ordered an investigation. I know that the CIA is already going forward with one. We have a gentleman down in Nicaragua who is on contract to the CIA, advising—supposedly on military tactics—the contras. And he drew up this manual. It was turned over to the agency head of the CIA in Nicaragua to be printed. And a number of pages were excised by that agency head there, the man in charge, and he sent it on up here to CIA, where more pages were excised before it was printed. But some way or other, there were 12 of the original copies that got out down there and were not submitted for this printing process by the CIA.

Surprised by Reagan's admission, one of the moderators, Geyer, asked for more details: 'Well, Mr. President, you are implying then that the CIA in Nicaragua is directing the contras there. I'd also like to ask whether having the CIA investigate its own manual in such a sensitive area is not sort of like sending the fox into the chicken coop a second time?' Reagan quickly reversed his position:

> I'm afraid I misspoke when I said a CIA head in Nicaragua. There's not someone there directing all of this activity. There are, as you know, CIA men stationed in other countries in the world and, certainly, in Central America. And so it was a man down there in that area that this was delivered to, and he recognized that what was in that manual was in direct contravention of my own Executive order, in December of 1981, that we would have nothing to do with regard to political assassinations.

Mondale's rebuttal foreshadowed the conclusions of the Tower Commission's investigation in the Iran-Contra affair, which was damning of Reagan's management style. He remarked: 'How can something this serious occur in an administration and have a President of the United States in a situation like this say he didn't know? A President must know these things. I don't know which is worse, not knowing or knowing and not stopping it'. Responding to Mondale's criticism of the mining of Nicaraguan harbours by the CIA, Reagan was again the debate performer who batted away Carter's claims about policy statements and intentions:

> I have so many things there to respond to, I'm going to pick out something you said earlier. You've been all over the country repeating something

that, I will admit, the press has also been repeating-that I believed that nuclear missiles could be fired and then called back. I never, ever conceived of such a thing. I never said any such thing ... How anyone could think that any sane person would believe you could call back a nuclear missile, I think is as ridiculous as the whole concept has been. So, thank you for giving me a chance to straighten the record. I'm sure that you appreciate that.

Following laughter from the audience, the debate moved on to the Soviet Union.[212] Reagan successfully backtracked on his prior comments about the CIA and did not answered Mondale's question, laughing it off and downplaying the significance of the issue. Nevertheless, Nicaragua remained a hostage to fortune. For Deaver, the key lesson from the first debate was that Reagan could not be over-managed—Reagan had to be allowed to Reagan. Recalling the occasion, he observed:

> [T]he first '84 re-election debate with [Walter] Mondale was a disaster, and it was because the [David] Gergens and the [Dick] Darmans of the world, who never had a lot of confidence in Ronald Reagan to begin with, decided—and Jim Baker went along with this—that we had to do the same thing we'd done in '80, in preparing him for the debates. Well, in '80 he'd never been President. In '84 he'd been President for four years. What they did was fill his computer with a whole bunch of facts instead of giving him broad themes, which is what he can do much better. In the second debate, I refused to allow debate preparation. I said, You just submit broad themes, and, of course, he hit a home run.[213]

Reagan's record and rhetoric about the Cold War had been a point of contention among his advisers while he prepared for the second debate. Concerned about a *New York Times* article on 16 October entitled 'Reagan Says No More Hard Line on Russia', Anthony Dolan (who served as a White House speechwriter for almost the entirety of the Reagan years) shared his thoughts with Baker, Deaver, and McFarlane.[214] For Dolan, any advice, such as that from Jack Matlock (then a White House adviser and future ambassador to the Soviet Union in 1987–1991) that Reagan should 'move away from his commitment to freedom—in the face of an aggressive Mondale who will push him on this point' would only cause 'serious damage' to his credibility and electoral support. Dolan argued that aspect of Reagan's brand was Churchillian: 'Twenty years from now, historians will look back at this—as they did at Churchill's warnings about Hitler or about the "Iron Curtain"—as the most significant foreign policy accomplishment of the Reagan Administration, and perhaps the critical reason for the loss of Soviet energy. Do not advise the President to retreat from this. He should claim credit for it'. In a reference to a widely popular children's television show, he further argued that Reagan should say at the debate: 'The world is not Mr. Rogers' Neighborhood and my opponent really doesn't understand that … It's true I've been honest about those dangers and been candid with the American people about our adversaries … History shows that when the Soviets know their counterparts have no illusions about them, they settle down to serious negotiating'. That same day, John Poindexter (deputy national security adviser, 1983–1985) sent a handwritten note to McFarlane: 'Bud, I really object to Dolan's inflammatory statement about Jack. Dolan doesn't understand the issues (or the President) and I doubt he ever will. You might want to call Dolan and tell him this kind of sniping and extremism doesn't help'.[215] In the debate, Reagan did not back away from his prior comments about the Soviet Union, but he did continue to emphasise a more pragmatic approach to easing Cold War tensions and the threat of nuclear war:

> I have said on a number of occasions exactly what I believe about the Soviet Union. I retract nothing that I have said. I believe that many of the things they have done are evil in any concept of morality that we have. But I also recognize that as the two great superpowers in the world, we have to live with each other. And I told Mr. Gromyko [minister for foreign affairs for the Soviet Union] … it was to their common interest, along with ours, to avoid a conflict and to attempt to save the world and remove the nuclear weapons. And I think that perhaps we established a little better understanding.

It was clear that some of those responsible for shaping Reagan's message in the campaign and his presidency generally disagreed with those who recognised the realities of international relations and opportunity for dialogues with the Soviet Union during a second Reagan term.

Reagan's campaign themes were codified by his concluding five-minute advertisement—'Unity'—where, sitting by a fireplace, he talked about his ideals and the achievements of his first term:

> There's been something special in this campaign. In the bright eyes of our young, I see America coming together again. They are what this election

is all about. They deserve a tomorrow when they can fly as high as their talents will take them. We're coming together again and building again. And across this shining land, we are happy to get together again. How can anyone doubt that our best days are yet to come?[216]

Writing in the *Washington Post*, David S. Broder argued that in 1984 presidential campaign, Reagan seized 'the banner of futurism for the GOP'.[217] Indeed, less than two months before election day, a *Washington Post-ABC News* poll showed that Americans believed they would be better off with a second term for Reagan 'by a 53–37 percent margin'. Reagan's campaign rhetoric had focused on values instead of any specific policy promises—a classic example of the truism that Americans campaign in poetry, yet govern in prose.[218] Reagan was re-elected by the largest ever electoral landslide: 525 Electoral College votes, and in doing so he won 49 states and the constitutionally irrelevant, but politically significant, popular vote with 59%. This was an extraordinary mandate. For Reagan, it was a cue for him and Nancy to spend some time together at the ranch.[219]

NOTES

1. Matthew Dickinson, 'How One President Spent His Year, Summarized in One Table: Ronald Reagan, 1984,' *Presidential Power*, 12 July 2014: https://sites.middlebury.edu/presidential power/2014/07/12/how-a-president-spends-his-year-in-one-table-ronald-reagan-1984/.
2. The American Presidency Project, "Seats in Congress Gained/Lost by the President's Party in Mid-Term Elections." Santa Barbara, CA: University of California. Available from the World Wide Web: https://www.presidency.ucsb.edu/node/332343/.
3. Memorandum, Richard B. Wirthlin to President Ronald Reagan, 'Political Challenges We Face in 1983 and Beyond,' 8 December 1982, James A Baker files, White House Staff Memoranda – Political Affairs (3) Box: 5, Ronald Reagan Library: https://www.reaganlibrary.gov/public/digitallibrary/smof/cos/bakerj ames/box-005/40-028-6914302-005-014-2016.pdf.
4. Ibid.
5. Ibid.

6. Report, 'The GOP Presidential Coalition of 1984,' author and date unknown: https://www.reaganlibrary.gov/public/digitalli brary/smof/cos/bakerjames/box-009/40-028-6914302-009-015-2016.pdf.
7. Ibid.
8. *Roper Center*, 'How Groups Voted in 1984': https://roperc enter.cornell.edu/how-groups-voted-1984.
9. David S. Broder, 'GOP Seeks Signs, Strategy In Thatcher's Election Stakes,' *The Charlotte Observer*, Thursday 9 June 1983.
10. Report, S. Anna Kondrates (Deputy Director of Research) and Vivianne Schneider (Issues Analyst), through William I. Greener III (Director of Communications) and Philip Kawior (Director of Research), to Frank J. Fahrenkopf Jr. (Chairman), June 20, 1983, 182559, C0167, WHORM: Subject File, Ronald Reagan Library.
11. Ibid.
12. Ronald Reagan, 'Address to the Nation on Defense and National Security,' 23 March 1983: https://www.reaganlibrary.gov/arc hives/speech/address-nation-defense-and-national-security.
13. Ibid.
14. Rick Atkinson, '"Star Wars" and the ASAT Projects: Wares and Whys of Space Defense,' *The Washington Post*, 23 June 1984: https://www.washingtonpost.com/archive/politics/1984/06/ 23/star-wars-and-the-asat-projects-wares-and-whys-of-space-def ense/94f37ecc-778d-4508-b834-e3200f9dafd9/.
15. Donald T. Regan, *For the Record: From Wall Street to Washington* (Arrow Books: California, 1988), 294.
16. Lou Cannon, 'Reagan, Calling U.S. Safer Than Before, Gives "Agenda for Peace,"' *Washington Post*, 26 January 1984: https://www.washingtonpost.com/archive/politics/1984/01/ 26/reagan-calling-us-safer-than-before-gives-agenda-for-peace/ 9281f896-cf97-40fa-88d2-2a4cc2fb0971/.
17. 'Memo to James Baker and Bud McFarlane re: Proposed Break-fast Meeting on Central America,' 23 July 1984, Ronald Reagan Library, James Baker Files, National Security Office: https:// www.reaganlibrary.gov/public/digitallibrary/smof/cos/bakerj ames/box-009/40-028-6914302-009-007-2016.pdf.
18. Ibid.

19. Defense Nuclear Agency, Atmospheric Effects Division, "Global Effects of Nuclear War," Briefing, February 1984, unclassified, National Security Archive: https://nsarchive.gwu.edu/doc ument/28223-document-4-defense-nuclear-agency-atmospheric-effects-division-global-effects; Lawrence Livermore Laboratory, "Global Effects of Nuclear War Study Project – First Quarterly Report January-March 1984." Prepared by George F Bing, 18 May 1984, unclassified, National Security Archive: https://nsa rchive.gwu.edu/document/28225-document-6-lawrence-liverm ore-laboratory-global-effects-nuclear-war-study-project.

20. Memorandum of Conversation, 'Summary of President's Meeting with British Opposition Neil Kinnock,' 14 February 1984, Secret. National Security Archive: https://nsarchive.gwu.edu/document/28224-document-5-memorandum-conversation-sum mary-presidents-meeting-british-opposition

21. Ronald Reagan, 'Address Before a Joint Session of the Congress on the State of the Union - January 1984,' 25 January 1984: https://www.reaganlibrary.gov/archives/speech/address-joint-session-congress-state-union-january-1984.

22. Ibid.

23. Ronald Reagan, 'Address to the Nation Announcing the Reagan-Bush Candidacies for Reelection,' 29 January 1984: https://www.reaganlibrary.gov/archives/speech/address-nation-announ cing-reagan-bush-candidacies-reelection.

24. Ibid.

25. Ronald Reagan, 'Remarks at Memorial Day Ceremonies Honoring an Unknown Serviceman of the Vietnam Conflict,' 28 May 1984: https://www.reaganlibrary.gov/archives/spe ech/remarks-memorial-day-ceremonies-honoring-unknown-ser viceman-vietnam-conflict.

26. Jonathan Fuerbringer, 'Reagan signs Bill to Cut Spending, Raise Taxes,' *The New York Times*, 19 July 1984: https://www.nyt imes.com/1984/07/19/business/reagan-signs-bill-to-cut-spe nding-raise-taxes.html.

27. Memorandum, Jim Lake to Mike Deaver, 'Reagan-Bush'84: The President's Authorized Campaign Committee,' 9 April 1984, Deaver, Michal: Files, Folder Title: Campaign 1984 (3), Box 67, Reagan Library: https://www.reaganlibrary.gov/public/digitalli brary/smof/dcos/deaver/box-067/40-137-7065200-067-006-2016.pdf.

28. Hedrick Smith, 'Reagan's Effort to Change Course of Government,' *The New York Times*, 23 October 1984, A26.
29. Hugh Sidey, 'The Presidency by Hugh Sidey: A Conversation with Reagan,' *Time*, 3 September 1984: https://content.time.com/time/subscriber/article/0,33009,951271,00.html.
30. "The Presidency," *We the People: An American Celebration, Pictorial History of the 50th American Presidential Inaugural and Events Leading Up to It* (Washington, D.C.: Presidential Inaugural Committee, 1985), 3.
31. Rudalevige. *The New Imperial Presidency*, 168.
32. Ryan J. Barilleaux, *The Post-Modern Presidency* (New York, NY: Praeger, 1988); C. Rimmerman, 'Review: The "Post-Modern Presidency. A New Presidential Epoch: A Review Essay,' *The Western Political Quarterly* 44:1 (1991), 221–238; Richard Rose, *The Post-Modern President* (Chatham, NJ: Chatham House Publishers, 1991).
33. Stephen Skowronek, *The Politics Presidents Make: Leadership from John Adams to Bill Clinton* (Cambridge, MA: Harvard University Press, 1993), 411. The other three types of presidencies, according to Skowronek's 'regime theory' of the presidency, include the 'affiliated' presidencies, the 'pre-emptive' presidents, and finally the 'disjunctive' president who precedes the 'reconstructive' president. Presidents such as John Quincy Adams, Herbert Hoover, and Jimmy Carter are considered disjunctive because their presidencies oversaw the final decay of the prevailing regime during which time it implodes after which the political order is reconstructed by the president who establishes a new regime in American politics.
34. Thomas. B. Edsall, 'The Fight Over How Trump Fits in With the Other 44 Presidents,' *The New York Times*, 15 May 2019: https://www.nytimes.com/2019/05/15/opinion/trump-history-presidents.html.
35. Ibid.
36. The White House, *Executive Order 12333 of Dec 4, 1981—United States Intelligence Activities* (Washington, D.C., 1981): https://dpcld.defense.gov/Portals/49/Documents/Civil/eo-12333-2008.pdf.
37. The White House. *Executive Order 12333 of Dec 4, 1981 – United States Intelligence Activities* (Washington, D.C., 1981):

https://www.archives.gov/federal-register/codification/execut
ive-order/12333.html.

38. Ibid. Andrew Rudalevige writes that presidents 'starting with Ronald Reagan aggressively used executive tools – from regulatory review to signing statements – to enhance their influence over bureaucratic outputs and avoid legislative dictation.' See: Andrew Rudalevige, '"The Contemporary Presidency": The Decline and Resurgence and Decline (and Resurgence?) of Congress: Charting a New Imperial Presidency,' *Presidential Studies Quarterly* 36:3 (2006), 510.

39. Anna Kitsmarishvili, 'The Rise of the Unilateral Executive,' *Global Tides* 10:8 (2016), 1: https://digitalcommons.pepperdine.edu/globaltides/vol10/iss1/8/.

40. Philip Taubman, 'Casey and His CIA on the Rebound,' *The New York Times*, 16 January 1983: https://www.nytimes.com/1983/01/16/magazine/casey-and-his-cia-on-the-rebound.html.

41. Todd R. Greentree, *The Origins of the "Reagan Doctrine Wars" in Angola, Central America, and Afghanistan* (Oxford: Oxford University Press, 2016); Bob Woodward, *Veil: The Secret Wars of the CIA, 1981–1987* (New York, NY: Simon & Schuster, 1987).

42. Greentree, *The Origins*, 202–203.

43. Ibid.

44. U.S. Congress, *H.R. 2760: A Bill to Amend the Intelligence Authorization Act for Fiscal Year 1983 to prohibit United States support for military or paramilitary operations in Nicaragua and to authorize assistance* (Washington, D.C., 1983): https://www.congress.gov/bill/98th-congress/house-bill/2760.

45. Joseph A. Ledford, *Thesis: The Iran-Contra Affair and the Cold War: A "Neat Idea" and the Reagan Doctrine* (Massachusetts, 2016). Ledford referred to the Iran-Contra scandal as the 'Reagan Doctrine fundamentally in action.'

46. Philip Taubman, 'The Reagan Doctrine,' *The New York Times*, 31 July 1983: https://www.nytimes.com/1983/07/31/weekin review/the-reagan-doctrine.html.

47. Byrne, *Iran-Contra*, 55–56.

48. Byrne, 135. Byrne writes that, 'Even though the events that constituted the Contra side of the Iran-Contra scandal did not begin to fully roll out until late 1984, when the administration

labored to sustain the war by going around the most restrictive Boland Amendment, the groundwork for those controversial activities was already in place.'

49. National Security Council, National Security Planning Group Minutes, "Subject: Central America," 25 June 1984, *National Security Archive*: https://nsarchive.gwu.edu/document/22302-01-nsc-national-security-planning-group-minutes.

50. Ibid.

51. Stuart M. Butler, Michal Sanera, and W. Bruce Weinrod, *Mandate for Leadership II: Continuing the Conservative Revolution by* (Heritage Foundation: Washington, D.C., 1984), 287.

52. Ronald Reagan, 'State of the Union Speech, March 13, 1980,' in K. Skinner, Annelise Anderson, and Martin Anderson (eds.), *Reagan: In His Own Hand* (New York, NY: Simon and Schuster, 2001), 477.

53. Robert W. Tucker, 'Reagan's Foreign Policy,' *The Council on Foreign Relations* 68:1 (1989), 13.

54. Letter from Davis R. Robinson, Legal Adviser, United States Department of State, to Prof. Edward Gordon, Chairman, Committee on Grenada, Section on International Law and Practice, American Bar Association (Feb. 10, 1984): https://core.ac.uk/download/pdf/216913139.pdf.

55. John Quigley, 'The United States Invasion of Grenada: Stranger than Fiction,' *The University of Miami Inter-American Law Review* 18:2 (1987), 273.

56. S. Chaudhurl, 'Invasion of Grenada,' *Economic and Political Weekly* 18:44 (1983), 1857.

57. Chaudhurl, 'Invasion of Grenada,' 1857.

58. E. Kenworthy, 'Grenada as Theatre,' *World Policy Journal* 1:3 (1984), 635–636.

59. S. L. Carter, 'The Constitutionality of the War Powers Resolution,' *Virginia Law Review* 70:1 (1984), 101.

60. Reagan, *An American Life*, 753.

61. Ibid.

62. Ibid.

63. Hedrick Smith, 'Reagan, in U.S., Says China Trip Advanced Ties,' *The New York* Times, 2 May 1984, A1.

64. Document 77, 'Notes Prepared by the President's Assistant for National Security Affairs (Carlucci).' *Foreign Relations of the*

United States, 1981–1988, Volume VI, Soviet Union, October 1986–January 1989, 390–391.

65. Ronald Reagan. 'Remarks Upon Returning From China,' 1 May 1984: https://www.reaganlibrary.gov/archives/speech/remarks-upon-returning-china.

66. Defense Intelligence Agency, 'Defense Estimative Brief: Nuclear Weapons in China,' 24 April 1984: https://nsarchive.gwu.edu/document/15931-document-17-defense-intelligence-agency-defense.

67. John D. Ehrlichman, 'Reagan's Challenge in China,' *The New York Times*, 30 March 1984: https://www.nytimes.com/1984/03/30/opinion/reagan-s-challenge-in-china.html.

68. Van Gosse, 'Ronald Reagan in Ireland, 1984: A Different Cold War?' *Journal of American Studies* 47:4 (2013), 1155.

69. Gosse, 'Ronald Reagan in Ireland, 1984: A Different Cold War?,' 1155.

70. Thomson, 'Presidential Travel and the Rose Garden Strategy,' 864–888.

71. Ronald Reagan, 'Address Before a Joint Session of the Irish National Parliament,' 4 June 1984: https://www.reaganlibrary.gov/archives/speech/address-joint-session-irish-national-parliament.

72. E. D. Dover, *Images, Issues, and Attacks: Television Advertising by Incumbents and Challengers in Presidential Elections* (Plymouth, UK: Lexington Books, 2006), 28–29.

73. Ronald Reagan, 'Remarks at a Ceremony Commemorating the 40th Anniversary of the Normandy Invasion, D-day,' 6 June 1984: https://www.reaganlibrary.gov/archives/speech/remarks-ceremony-commemorating-40th-anniversary-normandy-invasion-d-day.

74. Ronald Reagan, 'Remarks at a United States-France Ceremony Commemorating the 40th Anniversary of the Normandy Invasion, D-day,' 6 June 1984: https://www.reaganlibrary.gov/archives/speech/remarks-united-states-france-ceremony-commemorating-40th-anniversary-normandy.

75. Document 196, 'Note From the President's Assistant for National Security Affairs (McFarlane) to President Reagan,' Washington, 10 June 1984, *Foreign Relations of the United States, 1981–1988,*

Volume 1, Foundations of Foreign Policy: https://history.state.gov/historicaldocuments/frus1981-88v01/d196.

76. Ibid.

77. Reagan job approval rating for 29 June 1984–2 July 1984, data adapted from the Gallup Poll and complied by Gerhard Peters, accessed via, Gerhard Peters and John T. Woolley (eds.), *The American Presidency Project*, http://www.presidency.ucsb.edu/data/popularity.php?pres=40&sort=pop&direct=DESC&Submit=DISPLAY, 23 April 2018.

78. Cooper, *A Diplomatic Meeting*, 127–134.

79. Memorandum for the President, From: Robert C. McFarlane, Subject: Your European Trip: Bilateral Aspects, The Presidents" Trip to Europe: Ireland, UK and Normandy (1 of 6), 06/01/1984–06/10/1984, Box 20, Coordination, NSC, Office of Records, Ronald Reagan Presidential Library.

80. Ibid.

81. Hobart Rowen, 'Doubters Await Reagan at Summit: Reagan's Economic Outlook Likely to Be Challenged at Summit,' *Washington Post*, Monday 4 June 1984, A1.

82. PREM 19/1210: UKE Embassy to FCO, London Economic Summit, Telegram 1 June 1984, "Economic Summit: American Expectations."

83. Ibid.

84. 'London Economic Summit Conference Declaration,' 9 June 1984: https://www.reaganlibrary.gov/archives/speech/london-economic-summit-conference-declaration.

85. UKE Washington telegram to FCO ("US Public Reactions to the Summit") Monday 11 June 1984: http://margaretthatcher.org/document/145784.

86. Ronald Reagan, 'Informal Exchange With Reporters on Soviet Withdrawal From the 1984 Summer Olympic Games,' 9 May 1984: https://www.reaganlibrary.gov/archives/speech/informal-exchange-reporters-soviet-withdrawal-1984-summer-olympic-games.

87. Ronald Reagan, 'Remarks at a White House Ceremony on the 1984 Olympic Torch Relay,' 14 May 1984: https://www.reaganlibrary.gov/archives/speech/remarks-white-house-ceremony-1984-olympic-torch-relay.

88. Ronald Reagan, 'Remarks to United States Olympic Medal Winners in Los Angeles, California,' 13 August 1984: https://www.reaganlibrary.gov/archives/speech/remarks-united-states-olympic-medal-winners-los-angeles-california.
89. Ibid.
90. Michael Beschloss, 'The Ad That Helped Reagan Sell Good Times to an Uncertain Nation,' *The New York Times*, 7 May 2016: https://www.nytimes.com/2016/05/08/business/the-ad-that-helped-reagan-sell-good-times-to-an-uncertain-nation.html.
91. *Variety* Film Review: 'The Natural' Starring Robert Redford,' 31 December 1984: https://variety.com/1983/film/reviews/the-natural-1200425914/.
92. Broussard, *Ronald Reagan*, 147.
93. Remarks at Reagan-Bush Rally, September 19, 1984, Hammonton NJ: https://www.reaganlibrary.gov/archives/speech/remarks-reagan-bush-rally-hammonton-new-jersey.
94. Randall Bennett Woods, *Quest for Identity: America Since 1945* (Cambridge: Cambridge University Press, 2005), 457.
95. Kevin Baker, '"Welcome to Fear City" – the inside story of New York's civil war, 40 years on,' *The Guardian*, 18 May 2015: www.theguardian.com/cities/2015/may/18/welcome-to-fear-city-the-inside-story-of-new-yorks-civil-war-40-years-on.
96. This was a misquote. See: Sam Roberts, 'Infamous "Drop Dead" Was Never Said by Ford,' *New York Times*, 28 December 2006: www.nytimes.com/2006/12/28/nyregion/28veto.html. More detail on Ford refusal can be found at: Martin Tolchin, 'Bailout Barred, President's Plan Has Provision for Safety in Event of Default Ford Asserts He Would veto City Loan Guarantee,' *New York Times*, 30 October 1975: www.timesmachine.nytimes.com/timesmachine/1975/10/30/issue.html.
97. Rockwell, *Somebody's Watching Me*, track 1, 'Somebody's Watching Me', Motown, 1984.
98. Bruce Springsteen, *Born in the U.S.A.*, track 11, 'Dancing in the Dark,' Columbia, 1984.
99. Billy Joel, *Innocent Man*, track 2, 'An Innocent Man', Family Productions, Columbia, 1984.
100. Run-D.M.C., *Hard Times*, track 1, 'It's Like That,' Profile/Arista, 1984.

101. Cyndi Lauper, *She Bop*, track 5, 'She's So Unusual', Record Plant, 1983; Madonna, *Borderline*. track 2, 'Madonna', Sire Records / Warner Bros, 1983.
102. Tina Turner, *What's Love Got to Do With It*, track 2, 'Private Dancer', Capitol, 1984; Pointer Sisters, *Automatic*, track 2, and *I'm So Excited*, track 3, 'Break Out' (1984 re-release), Planet / RCA Records, 1984.
103. The Go-Gos, Head over Heels, 'Talk Show,' Sony, 1984; Kenny Loggins, *Footloose* (from the movie, *Footloose*, 1984).
104. Woods, *Quest, 457.*
105. Supertramp, *Brother Where You Bound*, track 5, 'Brother Where You Bound,' A&M, 1985. The news extracts may have been taken from a radio news report by Elmer Davis from 3 February 1946: www.historyonthenet.com/authentichistory/1946-1960/1-cworigins/19460203_Elmer_Davis-Russia_and_Greece-lyrics.html
106. *Red Dawn*, directed by John Milieus (United Artists, 1984).
107. As claimed by Swayze in the *Red Dawn* (1984) DVD extras featurette 'Red Dawn Rising' https://www.youtube.com/watch?v=GF_5kTPpFaU.
108. Scott Harrison, '7 of the Best Alternate Brat Pack Films' *Arrow-Films* (date unknown): https://www.arrowfilms.com/blog/features/7-of-the-best-alternate-brat-pack-films/.
109. *Red Dawn.*
110. *Red Dawn* (1984) John Milius, USA, screened by the Reagans at Camp David, 7 September 1984, 'Films Viewed by President and Mrs. Reagan': www.reaganlibrary.gov/reagans/reagan-administration/films-viewed-president-and-mrs-reagan.
111. Swayze: https://www.youtube.com/watch?v=GF_5kTPpFaU.
112. Janet Maslin, 'Film: '"Red Dawn" on World War III,' *New York Times*, 10 August 1984, C11: https://www.nytimes.com/1984/08/10/movies/film-red-dawn-on-world-war-iii.html.
113. Rita Kempley, 'Red Daw': Viewers Take Warning,' *The Washington Post*, 10 August 1984: www.washingtonpost.com/archive/lifestyle/1984/08/10/red-dawn-viewers-take-warning/e3e1781c-5548-45a4-9796-0bbe962b6d73/.
114. Gary Arnold, '"Dawn" of the Dud,' *The Washington Post*, 10 August 1984: https://www.washingtonpost.com/archive/lifestyle/1984/08/10/dawn-of-the-dud/d8d6a115-12e6-4118-852a-413af7b230f7/.

115. Aljean Harmetz, 'Some Groups Unhappy with New PG-13 Rating,' *New York Times, 13* August 1984, C20: https://www.nytimes.com/1984/08/13/arts/some-groups-unhappy-with-pg-13-film-rating.html.

116. Director John Milius in *Red Dawn* (1984) DVD extras featurette 'Red Dawn Rising': https://www.youtube.com/watch?v=GF_5kTPpFaU.

117. Ronald Reagan 1984 TV Ad: 'The Bear': https://www.youtube.com/watch?v=NpwdcmjBgNA.

118. Russia's connection with the symbol of a bear is not as clear cut as it would first appear, with the bear depicted in an often-unflattering light throughout folk tales. Early reference to the 'Russian bear' can be found in Shakespeare's *Macbeth* AIII, Sc4 *"What man dare, I dare: Approach thou like the rugged Russian bear"* with more emblematic use appearing in a caricature of Catherine II entitled *"The Russian Bear and Her Invincible Rider Encountering the British Legion"* published in April 1791 and then *"The Bear, the Bulldog, and the Monkey"* published in August 1812 as French troops were marching towards Moscow. In the image, Napoleon is portrayed as a monkey in the clutches of a bear and a bulldog. The bear was selected as the mascot for the 1980 Summer Olympic Games in Moscow, also known as 'Mishka'. Russians are more likely to choose the two-headed eagle as their national symbol (56% of those polled) whereas Americans would choose the bear (46% of those polled) (survey of 100 people in Russia and 100 in the USA conducted in 2009 and results given through a conference paper in 2010). See also: Anne M. Platoff, 'The "Forward Russia" Flag: Examining the Changing Use of the Bear as a Symbol of Russia,' *Raven: A Journal of Vexillology* 19 (2012), 99–126.

119. Martin Schram, 'Reagan Aides Bullish on 'The Bear' Ads,' *The Washington Post*, 2 November 1984: www.washingtonpost.com/archive/politics/1984/11/02/reagan-aides-bullish-on-the-bear-ads/aecf20e4-780b-49ac-8d08-07e93002798e/.

120. Ibid.

121. Dover, *Images*, 29.

122. Ibid, 30.

123. Ibid.

124. Janet Maslin, 'Murphy in Beverly Hills Cop,' *The New York Times*, 5 December 1984, C25: https://www.nytimes.com/1984/12/05/movies/film-murphy-in-beverly-hills-cop.html.

125. Indeed, villain Victor Maitland summarises Axel's home as '*Detroit Is a Very Violent City, Isn't it?*'. See: 'Beverly Hills Cop,' Scripts.com. STANDS4 LLC, 2023: https://www.scripts.com/script/beverly_hills_cop_3978.

126. Reagan Campaign Advertisement, 'Prouder, Stronger, Better,' 1984: https://www.youtube.com/watch?v=pUMqic2IcWA.

127. *The Natural*, directed by Barry Levinson (Tri-Star, 1984).

128. Michael Beschloss, 'The Ad that helped Reagan sell good times to an uncertain nation' *New York Times*, 7 May 2016: www.nytimes.com/2016/05/08/business/the-ad-that-helped-reagan-sell-good-times-to-an-uncertain-nation.html.

129. Aidan Lewis Dolby, *Hollywood Masculinities: Themes, Bodies and Ideologies in 1980s Hybrid Action Cinema* (MA thesis submitted to York St John University, 2019), 27: ray.yorksj.ac.uk/id/eprint/4477/1/DOLBY%20AIDAN%20FINAL%20THESIS.pdf.

130. Run-D.M.C., *Hard Times*, track 1, and *It's Like That*, track 6, 'Run-D.M.C.', Profile/Arista, 1984.

131. Ibid.

132. Reagan Youth, 'Young Anthems for the New Order,' track 4, *I Hate Hate, R Radical, 1984.*

133. Reagan Youth, 'Young Anthems for the New Order,' track 5, *Degenerated.*

134. Reagan Youth, 'Youth Anthems for the New Order'.

135. Luke Ottenhof, 'Rockin' in the Free World? Inside the Rightwing Takeover of Protest Music,' *The Guardian*, 13 April 2021: www.theguardian.com/music/2021/apr/13/right-wing-take-over-protest-music-bruce-springsteen-born-in-the-usa-american-politics.

136. 'Dancing in the Dark' was the last track recorded for the album when producer Jon Landau decided he wanted a 'single' for the album. After complaint from Springsteen ('I've written 70 songs. You want another one, you write it'), he went ahead and wrote the track overnight. It was recorded on 14 February 1984. See: Nancy Dunham, 'The Story Behind How "Dancing in the Dark" by Bruce Springsteen Came to Be,' American Songwriter,

2023: https://americansongwriter.com/the-story-behind-how-dancing-in-the-dark-by-bruce-springsteen-came-to-be/.

137. Bruce Springsteen, *Dancing in the Dark*, track 11, *Cover Me*, track 2, *My Hometown*, track 12, *Born in the USA*, track 1, 'Born in the U.S.A.,' Columbia, 1984.

138. Ronald Reagan, 'Remarks at Reagan-Bush Rally,' 19 September 1984, Hammonton NJ: www.reaganlibrary.gov/archives/spe ech/remarks-reagan-bush-rally-hammonton-new-jersey.

139. *Ghostbusters*, directed by Harold Ramis (Columbia, 1984), film screened by the Reagans at Camp David 14 July 1984, 'Films Viewed by President and Mrs. Reagan': www.reaganlibrary.gov/ reagans/reagan-administration/films-viewed-president-and-mrs-reagan.

140. Derek Robertson, 'The Weirdly Political Legacy of "Ghost-busters",' *Politico Magazine*, 21 November 2021: www.politico. com/news/magazine/2021/11/21/new-ghostbusters-afterlife-movie-politics-523082.

141. *Ghostbusters*, scene clip available here: www.youtube.com/watch? v=RjzC1Dgh17A.

142. *Ghostbusters*.

143. *Harold Ramis & Dam Ackroyd, Ghostbusters* (1984) (screenplay): https://scriptpdf.com/ghostbusters-1984-script-pdf/, 3.

144. *Ghostbusters*, scene clip available here: www.youtube.com/watch? v=N5C8C1WAywU.

145. Ramis and Ackroyd, *Ghostbusters*, 103.

146. *Ghostbusters*, scene clip available here: www.youtube.com/watch? v=N5C8C1WAywU.

147. 55 Central Park West was built by Schwartz and Gross in 1930. See: Christopher Gray, 'Streetscapes / 55 Central Park West; The Changing Colors of an Art Deco Landmark,' *The New York Times*, 11 July 1999: https://www.nytimes.com/1999/07/11/ realestate/streetscapes-55-central-park-west-the-changing-colors-of-an-art-deco-landmark.html.

148. Supertramp, *Better Days*, track 4, 'Brother Where You Bound,' A&M, 1985. See, www.youtube.com/watch?v=xE_dA479MCs: Reagan was one of politicians sampled, together with his oppo-nent Walter Mondale, and both running mates: Ferraro and Bush.

84   J. COOPER ET AL.

149. *The Natural* was screened by the Reagans at Camp David 12 May 1984, 'Films Viewed by President and Mrs. Reagan': www.reaganlibrary.gov/reagans/reagan-administration/films-viewed-president-and-mrs-reagan.
150. *All of Me*, directed by Carl Reiner (Universal, 1984).
151. There is little to verify that this was sung in Mandarin, Cantonese, or even Shanghainese or Manchu. One account suggests '*Kate Capshaw was singing badly-pronounced standard Chinese.*' The translation of what she made it to film, by a native speaker and translator, is interesting: https://youtu.be/f4bNusi9yAA His comments summarize the attempt: '*a curious study to the past, a byproduct [sic] of the shadow of linguistic imperialism and Hollywood whitewashing*'.
152. *Gunga Din*, directed by George Stevens (RKO Radio Pictures, 1939), film viewed 6 January 1984, 'Films Viewed by President and Mrs. Reagan': www.reaganlibrary.gov/reagans/reagan-administration/films-viewed-president-and-mrs-reagan.
153. This followed the interest in Egypt throughout the 1920s, following the uncovering of Tutankhamun's tomb, which of course provided the setting for the first Indiana Jones film *Raiders of the Lost Ark*, which was directed by Stephen Spielberg and released in 1981.
154. *Romancing the Stone*, directed by Robert Zemeckis (20th Century Fox, 1984), screened by the Reagans at Camp David, 11 May 1984, 'Films Viewed by President and Mrs. Reagan': www.reaganlibrary.gov/reagans/reagan-administration/films-viewed-president-and-mrs-reagan.
155. *Greystoke: The Legend of Tarzan*, directed Hugh Hudson (Warner Bros, 1984), screened by the Reagans at Camp David, 3 May 1984, 'Films Viewed by President and Mrs. Reagan': www.reaganlibrary.gov/reagans/reagan-administration/films-viewed-president-and-mrs-reagan.
156. *The Karate Kid*, directed by John G. Avildsen (Columbia Pictures, 1984), screened by the Reagans at Camp David, 30 June 1984, 'Films Viewed by President and Mrs. Reagan': www.reaganlibrary.gov/reagans/reagan-administration/films-viewed-president-and-mrs-reagan.
157. Jeffords, *Hard Bodies*, 179.

158. Ronald Reagan, 'Remarks at a Ceremony Commemorating the 40th Anniversary of the Normandy Invasion, D-day,' 6 June 1984: https://www.reaganfoundation.org/media/128809/normandy.pdf.

159. Bret E. Carroll, *American Masculinities: A Historical Encyclopaedia*, 1st ed. (California: Sage Publications, 2003), 98. See also: *Roger and Me*, directed by Michael Moore (Warner Bros, 1988).

160. David Mamet, *Glengarry Glen Ross* (London: Methuen, 1984).

161. *Indiana Jones and the Temple of Doom*, directed by Stephen Spielberg (Paramount, 1984).

162. Letter to the Editor, Bill Youmans, 'A New Model of Masculinity,' *New York Times*, 3 March 2018: https://www.nytimes.com/2018/03/03/opinion/sunday/boys-men-masculinity.html.

163. In *Hellcats of the Navy* (directed by Nathan Juran in 1957), Reagan took the lead role as Commander Casey Abbot, skipper of the USS Starfish.

164. In *Desperate Journey* (directed by Raoul Walsh in 1942), Reagan took a lead role as the '*half Jersey, half American*' Flying Officer, Johnny Hammond.

165. *Cattle Queen of Montana* (directed by Allan Dwan in 1954) was the last film Reagan screened while in office, but it is also referenced in *Back to the Future* (1985).

166. *Law and Order*, directed by Nathan Juran (1953).

167. Charles Bramesco, '"They Created a False Image": How the Reagans Fooled America,' *The Guardian*, 12 November 2020: https://www.theguardian.com/tv-and-radio/2020/nov/12/the-reagans-showtime-docuseries.

168. There were four "Brass" Bancroft films: *Secret Service of the Air* (1939) Noel M. Smith, USA, *Code of the Secret Service* (1939) Noel M. Smith USA, *Smashing the Money Ring* (1939) Terry O. Morse USA, and *Murder in the Air* (1940) Lewis Seller USA.

169. Trailer for Noel. M. Smith *Code of the Secret Service* (1939): www.youtube.com/watch?v=Sv-VGyS5a7w.

170. Zack Nauth, 'Fan Who Saved Life of President to Get His Reward Today,' *Los Angeles Times*, 15 February 1985: www.latimes.com/archives/la-xpm-1985-02-15-mn-3221-story.html.

171. Jack Dempsey, 1926: www.cmgww.com/sports/dempsey/quotes/.

172. Ronald Reagan, 'Remarks at a White House Meeting with Members of the American Business Conference,' 13 March 1985: https://www.reaganlibrary.gov/archives/speech/remarks-white-house-meeting-members-american-business-conference.

173. Note for Michael K. Deaver from Richard G. Darman, 'Follow-up RE Baker-Deaver-Darman-Spencer Meeting of 7/16/84,' 16 July 1984, Deaver, Michal: Files, Folder Title: Campaign 1984 (3), Box 67, Reagan Library: https://www.reaganlibrary.gov/public/digitallibrary/smof/dcos/deaver/box-067/40-137-706 5200-067-006-2016.pdf.

174. See, for instance: Richard Halloran, 'Reagan as Military Commander,' *The New York Times*, 15 January 1984: https://www.nytimes.com/1984/01/15/magazine/reagan-as-military-commander.html.

175. Halloran, 'Reagan as Military Commander.'

176. Reagan Foundation, [Video File] '1984 Presidential Candidate Debate: President Reagan and Walter Mondale – 10/21/84': https://www.youtube.com/watch?v=EF73k5-Hiqg.

177. Richard Reeves, 'The Ideological Election,' *The New York Times*, 19 February 1984: https://www.nytimes.com/1984/02/19/magazine/the-ideological-election.html

178. Reeves, 'The Ideological Election.'

179. Hedrick Smith, 'One Campaign Issue Dominates: The Leadership of Ronald Reagan,' *The New York Times*, 30 January 1984: https://www.nytimes.com/1984/01/30/us/one-campaign-issue-dominates-the-leadership-of-ronald-reagan.html.

180. David S. Broder, 'Election'84,' *Washington Post*, 23 September 1984: https://www.washingtonpost.com/archive/politics/1984/09/23/election-84/09f03ed0-bfad-4bec-8505-6817b3e63306/.

181. Stephen Skowronek (ed.), *Presidential Leadership in Political Time: Reprise and Reappraisal* (Lawrence, KS: University Press of Kansas, 2020), 11: 'Presidential agency—the efficacy of political action in the presidential office—is primarily a legitimation problem. Incumbents are engaged in a contest to control the meaning of actions that are inherently disruptive of the status quo ante. The president who successfully solves this problem will wield a form of authority that is difficult to resist; and those who follow in the office will be constrained in their own efforts by the new

terms of legitimate national government secured by their predecessor.' Reagan's ability to align his definition over the actions he had undertaken in his project to renew presidential power, delimit the power of the federal government within the economy, and to effectively frame foreign policy as an issue of morality was thus well recognised in 1984.

182. Walter F. Mondale, Address Accepting the Presidential Nomination at the Democratic National Convention in San Francisco Online by Gerhard Peters and John T. Woolley, *The American Presidency Project* https://www.presidency.ucsb.edu/node/216667.

183. Ibid.

184. Dover, *Images*, 31. (The Republicans had transformed 'Reaganomics' from a term of derision into one that signalled economic success. This was obviously in contrast to the 'Mondalenomics' economic programme, which Walter Mondale, the Democrat nominee and Carter's Vice President, proposed. For the Republicans, 'Mondalenomics' was the term of derision that could be used politically.)

185. Republican Party Platforms, Republican Party Platform of 1984 Online by Gerhard Peters and John T. Woolley, The American Presidency Project https://www.presidency.ucsb.edu/node/273427.

186. Ibid.

187. Billy Joel, *Uptown Girl*, track 6, 'An Innocent Man', Family Productions/Columbia, 1984.

188. Official music video to *Uptown Girl* on Billy Joel's YouTube channel: www.youtube.com/watch?v=hCuMWrfXG4E.

189. Jim Jacobs' and Warren Casey's *Grease* opened in Chicago in 1971, Broadway in 1972, and the movie was released in 1978. The story was set in 1959.

190. 1984 Republican National Convention Film: www.youtube.com/watch?v=Z6XDMQPtQKw.

191. Michael Beschloss, 'The Ad that Helped Reagan Sell Good Times to an Uncertain Nation' *New York Times*, May 7 2016: www.nytimes.com/2016/05/08/business/the-ad-that-helped-reagan-sell-good-times-to-an-uncertain-nation.html.

192. For example, see this article from the New York City bar: https://www2.nycbar.org/htmlemail/SLFC/SpeakingTips forAttorneysOctober2013.pdf.

193. Ken Khachigian, quoted in Josh Mankiewicz, 'The Great Communicator,' *NBC News*, 6 June 2005: https://www.nbc news.com/id/wbna5146180.

194. See: Ida Zeitlin, *Photoplay, Movie Mirror*, January 1942, 30–31 and 77: https://archive.org/details/photoplay120phot/page/n37/mode/2up and https://archive.org/download/photoplay 120phot/photoplay120phot.pdf.

195. Ronald Reagan, 1984 Republican National Convention film, accessed via: https://www.youtube.com/watch?v=Z6XDMQ PtQKw [c.09:16–11:04].

196. Reagan, Convention Film: https://www.youtube.com/watch?v= Z6XDMQPtQKw.

197. Unnamed interviewee, Convention Film: https://www.youtube. com/watch?v=Z6XDMQPtQKw.

198. Reagan, Convention Film: https://www.youtube.com/watch?v= Z6XDMQPtQKw.

199. Ronald Reagan, Remarks Accepting the Presidential Nomination at the Republican National Convention in Dallas, Texas Online by Gerhard Peters and John T. Woolley, The American Presidency Project https://www.presidency.ucsb.edu/node/261945.

200. Franklin D. Roosevelt, Address at the Democratic State Convention, Syracuse, N.Y. Online by Gerhard Peters and John T. Woolley, The American Presidency Project https://www.presid ency.ucsb.edu/node/209137.

201. Ronald Reagan, Remarks Accepting the Presidential Nomination at the Republican National Convention in Dallas, Texas Online by Gerhard Peters and John T. Woolley, *The American Presidency Project* https://www.presidency.ucsb.edu/node/261945.

202. Ibid.

203. Bernard Weinraub, 'Mondale is Buoyed by His Success in First Debate,' *The New York Times*, 12 October 1984, B8.

204. Howell Raines, 'Reagan and Mondale Debate; Clash on Deficit, Social Issues,' *The New York Times*, 8 October 1984, A1.

205. Ronald Reagan, Debate Between the President and Former Vice President Walter F. Mondale in Louisville, Kentucky Online by

Gerhard Peters and John T. Woolley, *The American Presidency Project* https://www.presidency.ucsb.edu/node/217267.

206. Ibid.
207. Douglas Brinkley (ed.), Ronald Reagan, *The Reagan Diaries* (New York: HarperCollins, 2007), Saturday 6 October–Sunday 7 October 1984, 271.
208. Reagan, *Diaries*, Monday 8 October 1984, 271.
209. Ronald Reagan, Debate Between the President and Former Vice President Walter F. Mondale in Kansas City, Missouri Online by Gerhard Peters and John T. Woolley, *The American Presidency Project* https://www.presidency.ucsb.edu/node/217277
210. Ibid.
211. 'The Final Debate,' *The National Review*, 16 November 1984, 36:22, 16–17.
212. Ibid.
213. Michael Deaver, Ronald Reagan Oral History Project, 12 September 2002, Miller Center, University of Virginia: https://millercenter.org/the-presidency/presidential-oral-histories/michael-deaver-oral-history.
214. Document 207, Memorandum From the Special Assistant to the President and White House Chief Speechwriter (Dolan) to the White House Chief of Staff (Baker), the Assistant to the President and Deputy to the White House Chief of Staff (Darman), the White House deputy chief of staff (Deaver), and the President's Assistant for National Security Affairs (McFarlane), Washington, 17 October 1984: https://history.state.gov/historicaldocuments/frus1981-88v01/d207.
215. Ibid.
216. Dover, *Images*, 32.
217. David S. Broder, 'Reagan's Imported Tory Tactics,' *The Washington Post*, Sunday 16 September 1984, Final Edition, B7.
218. Quote attributed to Mario Cuomo (Democrat and governor of New York, 1983–1994). Cited by Elizabeth Kolbert, 'Postscript: Mario Cuomo (1932–2015),' The New Yorker, 1 January 2015: https://www.newyorker.com/news/news-desk/postscript-mario-cuomo.
219. Reagan, *Diaries*, 7 November 1984, 277.

Conclusion

Abstract This concluding chapter revisits the key claims of the overall work. It summarises Reagan's impact on American politics, policy-making, and popular culture. The extent of Reagan's popularity at the time and more recently are both explored. Similarly, the reaction of some other world leaders to the 1984 election result is considered, alongside how Reagan has been cited and utilised by his successors in American politics. The chapter identifies the importance of Reagan to the Republican Party as its 'party elder' and how the Democrats responded to the popularity of the 'Gipper'.

Keywords Reagan's legacy · New Democrats · Polling · International reactions · Obama · Barack

The 1984 presidential election result was an endorsement of the Reagan campaign team's approach. However, it was also an endorsement of the Reagan 'brand'. Regardless of the calculated ad copy, the carefully planned vox pops and D-Day appearances, Reagan was a well-trained actor, still interested in the craft, and knowledgeable, about movie culture in a decade in which the movie still mattered, and it was this quality that was the re-election team's decisive advantage. Speaking to the American people became, in a sense, an honest exchange for him, and when

© The Author(s), under exclusive license to Springer Nature Switzerland AG 2024
J. Cooper et al., *Ronald Reagan's 1984,*
https://doi.org/10.1007/978-3-031-53677-9_3

he felt that, it would appear that they sensed it too. The 1980s was a movie era of 'average Joes' forced into difficult circumstances, of reluctant heroes, guys next door who had to get a job done. Heroes were genuine, blue-collar men, some even finding that they were shoeless and firing a machine gun at a helicopter (John McClane being the perfect example of the accidental, reluctant hero in 1988s *Die Hard*). Of course, voters consider the geopolitics, domestic policies, and political manoeuvrings of any incumbent when assessing their record. However, in 1984, it was Reagan's perceived honesty in his television appearances that inspired the trust—not only in him but also in a previously beleaguered political establishment—that propelled voters to the ballot box in 1984. Reagan continues to evoke strong emotions, even from those who are too young to remember his tenure. A glance at the scores of comments under any of his 1984 campaign videos currently on *YouTube* will provide a reader with ample evidence that he still represents a halcyon period in the minds of many that commenters—one with a 'real' president. When Reagan first won the presidency in 1980, four-fifths of Americans believed that the United States was not working for all Americans, with three-quarters also thinking that the past was better than the future. Upon Reagan's re-election, two-fifths of Americans believed that the country was being run for the benefit of all, with half of those polled now looking optimistically to the future. Reagan had come to embody the best if American values and traditions.[1] Americans were certainly more optimistic in 1984 compared to four years earlier. 74% of them believed that the country was going in the right direction (either fairly well or very well), whereas in 1980 this figure was 32%.[2]

Even *The Goldbergs*, a sitcom based in a 1980s of nostalgia, noted the significance of the 1984 presidential election in the national consciousness. For instance, there was the following exchange between the mother, Beverly, who was campaigning locally for Reagan, and the daughter, Erica, who was supporting Mondale,

> *Erica*: My God! What horrible thing is happening in my house right now?
> *Beverly*: Something glorious. Your mother is going to single-handedly get The Gipper re-elected.
> *Erica*: You can't get Reagan re-elected just to spite me.
> *Beverly*: Oh, I can and I will. I will change the course of history just to show you how clue-ful I am.[3]

CONCLUSION 93

While Beverly Goldberg sought to change the course of history, the record of Reaganism is one of paradoxes. Reagan looked to scale back the national state but ended up consolidating the existence of key entitlements, notably social security. He promised to restore balanced budgets but ran the largest peacetime deficits in U.S. history up to that point. After promising and delivering tax cuts in 1981, the president raised taxes in 1982, 1983, 1984, and 1986 because of concerns about the federal budgetary deficit concerns. A final paradox is that Reagan's presidency restored popular confidence in the Federal government, which was, of course, the institution that he declared to be the problem and not the solution in his first inaugural address.[4] Erica Goldberg's support for Mondale was not typical of younger Americans. In 1984, Reagan was re-elected with the support of most of every age group, including 61% of voters aged 18–24 and 57% of those in the 25–29 age bracket.[5] In contrast, in recent years, young Americans have proven to be a crucial component of the Democrat's electoral support.[6] Reagan certainly made every effort to capture of support of young people as part of his campaign's strategy to own the future for the G.O.P.:

> For me, a vivid recollection … will be from a whistlestop train tour through Ohio in that historic car that once carried Franklin Roosevelt, Harry Truman, and Dwight Eisenhower across America. America had a smile in her heart that day. At each stop and through each community, whether gathered on their sidewalks, back lawns, or the plowed fields of their farms, again and again it was the young people I remembered -- Cub Scouts in blue shirts and bright yellow kerchiefs, high school bands, college crowds, and little girls perched atop their dads' shoulders. Well, they and millions more like them are what this election is all about.[7]

This study made three claims about Ronald Reagan's 1984. Re-election consolidated his grip and influence on the Republican Party. Reagan was no longer the politician who failed to take his party's nomination from President Gerald Ford in 1976. He was now the model against which all aspiring Republicans would be compared. Until, arguably, Donald Trump, the G.O.P. was the party of Reagan. After all, he was the only 'party elder' for contemporary American conservatives. Eisenhower's time in office was from a bygone generation of black and white news coverage. Despite his own landslide re-election in 1972, Nixon was *person non grata*. Bush Sr. failed to secure re-election, ushering in two terms of

94 J. COOPER ET AL.

Bill Clinton, while his son was a divisive figure following the invasion of, and war in, Iraq, after 2003. In the 2012 Republican presidential primaries, Newt Gingrich (speaker of the U.S. House of Representatives, 1995–1997) used Reagan's name fifty-five times in one debate, with the eventual nominee, Mitt Romney, criticising him for exaggerating the extent of his relationship with the fortieth president.[8] In addition to the beloved Reagan record in office and claim for him to have won the Cold War, Reagan remained the guiding presence in terms of philosophy, rhetoric, and policy when the Republican presidential primaries began in 2015.[9] Even Clinton famously declared in his 1996 state of the union speech that 'the era of big government is over', as part of a triangular politicking, with instead Americans now being in an 'era of working together as a community, as a team, as one America, with all of us reaching across these lines that divide us … we have to reach across it to find common ground'.[10] In turn, Reaganism was reflected in American popular culture during the 1980s. Academic ghost-hunters turned themselves in self-reliant capitalists. An archaeologist assumed a second identity away from the lecture theatre, looking for artefacts in an entrepreneurial spirit to secure fortune and glory for the museum attached to his college. Heroic Autobots battled evil Decepticons over energy reserves while preserving freedom for human beings.[11] It was also clear that Reagan of 1984 would approach the Cold War in a different way compared to his first term. Following the election results, Helmut Kohl, the chancellor of West Germany (including a united Germany, 1982–1998), believed that the president 'was obviously now reading and willing to take sensible steps towards the Soviet Union' who also now 'seemed ready to respond'.[12] Likewise, Sir Oliver Wright, the British ambassador to the United States (1982–1986), briefed London:

> For the Reagan of 1984 is already distinctly different from the Reagan of 1981, in playing up the need to improve the atmosphere, and the content, of the superpower dialogue. Cynics impute merely electoral motives: I do not … Having devoted his first term to making America strong, he will wish to devote the second to promoting peace, democracy and prosperity.[13]

This was evident during Thatcher's meeting with Reagan at Camp David in December 1984.[14] The prime minister reported that, after her recent meeting Gorbachev, she believed him to be 'an unusual kind of Russian' who 'was less constrained in what he said than other Soviet leaders'. Thatcher explained that in the meeting, her priority had been to persuade him 'the United States was sincere in wanting arms reductions'. In return, Reagan offered an account of how he had told Gromyko that 'the Soviet Union and United States each perceived themselves to be under threat from the other and therefore needed to establish mutual confidence' and wanted to work towards a world without nuclear weapons.[15]

Reagan's campaign sought to capture the future for the Republican Party. It did so by looking back at the failings of the Carter era and offering an optimistic outlook on the American future albeit based on a nostalgic understanding of a national past. Just like for Marty McFly going back to the future meant a return from 1955 to 1985, the oldest president in American history continued to promise leadership that had been forged in the 1950s and then tried and tested during the long 1960s.[16] Reagan's America was the future.

Reagan's filmography offers further insights into his ability to cultivate a popular coalition of support. In *Desperate Journey* (1942), the potential stands out even then. As captured Allied bomber crew member Johnny Hammond being interrogated about supercharging air engines, he convincingly rattles through a stream of nonsense terms in order to successfully manoeuvre himself close enough to knock out the questioning German officer, thereby heroically facilitating the escape of him and his fellow prisoners. This was a work of great communication from the future 'Great Communicator'.

> It's done with a thermothrokkle. ...A thermothrokkle, amphilated through a dallagalliter. Of course this is made possible because the durnadein has a frenner coupling. ...Well I knew you wouldn't, but if I'd a told you before the ancellmeter on the other side prenulates the canoodess spell hapulace. And that's the entire secret, there you have it. ...Well maybe I could make it more clear if I drew a diagram. ...You see there's three things you gotta understand. As I said before, the dallagalliter which is amphilated by the thermothrokkle and it is made possible by its connection with the frenner coupling of the durnedein. Well even at cruising speed naturally the canoodess spell hapulace is prenulated by the ancellmeter. Makes no difference, you could just be takin' off, snowin' or rainin' any pilot'll tell you that the altitude – ten, twenty, thirty, forty thousand feet...[17]

Reagan's electoral coalition was a combination of the demographics targeted by his campaign. He won the support of all groupings—male, female, household incomes, age ranges—and across all regions—with the exception of support from African-Americans (9%), Hispanics (34%), and those with an annual income of less than $12,500 (46%). However, Reagan was still supported by 26% of Democrats, 64% of independent voters, and 29% and 54% of liberals and moderates, respectively.[18] These statistics contribute to our understanding why 1984 was a mixed success for the Republican Party. The G.O.P retained control of the U.S. Senate (albeit losing this in the 1986 midterms), but despite gaining 16 seats in the U.S. House of Representatives, the Democrats enjoyed a popular vote national lead of over 5% and maintained control of the House. Likewise, the Republicans only gained a single Governorship in the gubernatorial elections.[19] Reagan's coat tails were long, but not long enough to break the impasse of divided government. Indeed, the Democrats would achieve such a feat in 1992, when Bill Clinton won the presidency and his party held control of Congress until 1994. George W. Bush's Republican Party controlled both the White House and Congress for two years after the 2003 midterms, and then it was the Democrats' turn for two years following the election of Barack Obama as president in 2008. Therefore, there was no great Reagan realignment akin to the more permanent coalition created by FDR and his New Deal. Nonetheless, Reagan's legacy—consolidated by the 1984 campaign— meant that Evangelical voters found for themselves a permanent political home in the Republican Party, while most young voters who supported Reagan would remain conservatives and support the G.O.P, helping to create the '50/50' partisan divided in contemporary American politics. Likewise, Reagan's optimistic brand of conservatism proved to be so electorally popular that it led to the political space for more pragmatic 'New Democrats' to have the opportunity to offer their party as an alternative to the Republicans after the 'Gipper' left the White House.[20]

Nonetheless, Reagan's re-election was an achievement that consolidated his legacy in American politics. Wright informed London that 'the result was a resounding vote of confidence ... for Reagan the man'.[21] For Wright, Reagan's success was inevitable: 'America is at peace abroad and with itself. Americans are feeling good about themselves and about a President in whom they see reflected the virtues that they like to feel they have: self-reliance, belief in family and religion, patriotism ... It was a victory of the 3P: peace, prosperity and personality'.[22] The United States was changing. As Wright observed, Reagan's campaign was in touch with economic structural developments away 'from the smokestack

CONCLUSION   97

to the high-tech and service industries ... The West has not only been won, but the Western ethos has won'. Moreover, the South's support for Reagan represented a 'seal of authenticity' in this 'shift in Presidential voting habits'. For Wright, the Democrats would 'have to change its spots and find new leaders with new ideas representative of the America of the present and future' with Senator Gary Hart 'a harbinger' of this development.[23] Reagan is one of only a handful of Republican presidents to have won and served two full terms in the White House (the others being Ulysses S. Grant, Dwight Eisenhower and George W. Bush). Even if Donald Trump were to return to the White House, it would be more akin to Grover Cleveland's stint as both the 22nd and 24th president of the United States. Reagan's comeback to Mondale in the second debate, espousing the virtues of age and wisdom, is consistently ranked as one of the most memorable debate moments in electoral debates.[24] Four year later, with Reagan unable to seek a third term, his vice president, George H. W. Bush, would even 'win one for the Gipper'.[25] Despite delivering a disappointing keynote speech at the 1988 Democratic National Convention, it was Bush's victory in 1988 that expedited Clinton's emergence as the key figure in the Democratic Leadership Conference that sought to reverse Republican success in national elections. The Democrats changed because of the Gipper, taking Clinton from the Governor's Mansion in Arkansas to the White House.[26] As noted previously, Reagan was viewed by older Americans to have been the best president of their lifetime. He was first and second choice for 36% of the 'silent' generation, 45% of baby boomers, and 43% of Gen X respondents. Clinton was a close second for the boomer and silent generations (35% and 42%, respectively), before leading among Gen X (57%, albeit Reagan second place) and comfortably the best president for millennials (61% first or next choice, with Reagan at 8%, behind Obama, Bush Jr and even marginally behind Bush Sr.).[27] While Americans across all demographic remain keen on pop music today, over half of them would have more sympathy for the message of music artists from the 1980s that they would for Reagan.[28]

This study began with remarks about the forty-fourth president of the United States and his own quest for presidential greatness. Reagan fulfilled the criteria that Brands explained to Obama for how to be considered a major presidential figure: by winning two terms and influencing American political discussion. In January 2008, at the beginning of his own campaign to win the White House for the first time, Obama identified Reagan as a transformational figure in American history:

He put us on a fundamentally different path because the country was ready for it. I think they felt like, you know, with all the excesses of the 60s and the 70s, and government had grown and grown, but there wasn't much sense of accountability in terms of how it was operating. I think people just tapped into -- he tapped into what people were already feeling, which was, we want clarity, we want optimism, we want a return to that sense of dynamism and entrepreneurship that had been missing.[29]

Similarly, William Buckley (conservative public intellectual and founder of the National Review) remarked of Reagan after meeting him in in the 1960s: 'Reagan is indisputably a part of America, and he may become a part of American history'.[30] 1984 was the pivotal year. The Reagan franchise was firmly established, and Reaganism would define the Republican Party and American politics for a generation.

NOTES

1. Woods, *Quest*, 458.
2. *Roper Center*, '1984 Presidential Election': https://roperc enter.cornell.edu/1984PresidentialElection, and '1980 Presidential Election': https://ropercenter.cornell.edu/1980PresidentialEl ection.
3. *The Goldbergs*, 'Just Say No,' Season 2, Episode 20, 15 April 2015: https://tvquot.es/the-goldbergs/just-say-no/.
4. For a more extensive discussion about Reagan's overall record and its contradictions, see, for instance: Morgan, *Reagan*, 315–333; Broussard, *Ronald Reagan*, 179–188; Andrew E Busch, 'Three Decades of Reaganism,' in Charles W. Dunn (ed.), *The Enduring Reagan* (Lexington, KY: University Press of Kentucky, 2009), 119–140; Steven F. Hayward, 'Is the "Age of Reagan" Over?', in *The Enduring Reagan*, 141–156; and, Hugh Heclo, 'The Mixed Legacies of Ronald Reagan,' *Presidential Studies Quarterly* 38: 4 (2008), 555–574.
5. Roper Center, 'How Groups Voted in 1984.'
6. In 2018, the Democrats held a 27 percent advantage ahead of the Republicans among millennial voters. See: *Pew Research Center*, 'Trends in party affiliation among demographic groups,' 20 March 2018: https://www.pewresearch.org/politics/2018/03/ 20/1-trends-in-party-affiliation-among-demographic-groups/.

7. Ronald Reagan, 'Address to the Nation on the Eve of the Presidential Election,' 5 November 1984: https://www.reaganlibrary.gov/archives/speech/address-nation-eve-presidential-election.
8. Peter Grier, 'Was Newt Gingrich Really All That Close to Ronald Reagan?,' *The Christian Science Monitor*, 25 January 2012: https://www.csmonitor.com/USA/Politics/The-Vote/2012/0125/Was-Newt-Gingrich-really-all-that-close-to-Ronald-Reagan.
9. See, for instance: Perry Bacon Jr., 'Despite New Challenges, GOP Still Looks to Reagan,' NBC News, 16 September 2015: https://www.nbcnews.com/meet-the-press/party-reagan-must-grapple-world-far-different-one-he-lead-n428336. For an excellent study about the 'third way' in American (and British) politics, see: Richard Carr, *March of the Moderates: Bill Clinton, Tony Blair, and the Rebirth of Progressive Politics* (London: I.B. Taurus, 2019).
10. Bill Clinton, 'State of the Union Address,' 23 January 1996: https://clintonwhitehouse4.archives.gov/WH/New/other/sotu.html.
11. The original animated television series based on the *Transformers* toy line aired in 1984.
12. No.10 record of conversation ("Anglo-German relations: Prime Minister's telephone call with Chancellor Kohl"), 28 November 1984: https://www.margaretthatcher.org/document/201478.
13. Ambassador Wright despatch to Howe ("1984 US Presidential Election Result: What Will Reagan Do?"), 6 November 1984: https://www.margaretthatcher.org/document/233123.
14. No.10 minute ("Record of a meeting between the Prime Minister and President Reagan at Camp David on 22 December 1984 at 1030 hours") [tête-à-tête on Gorbachev, SDI], 22 December 1984: https://www.margaretthatcher.org/document/136436.
15. Ibid. For the relationship between Gorbachev, Reagan, and Thatcher, see: Archie Brown, *The Human Factor: Gorbachev, Reagan, and Thatcher and the End of the Cold War* (Oxford: Oxford University Press, 2020). For a record of Thatcher's first meeting with Gorbachev in December 1984, see: No.10 record of conversation (MT-Gorbachev), 16 December 1984: https://www.margaretthatcher.org/document/233558.
16. For the 'long 1960s,' see, for instance: Arthur Marwick, 'The Cultural Revolution of the Long Sixties: Voices of Reaction, Protest, and Permeation,' *The International History Review* 27:4

(2005), 780–806; M. J. Heale, 'The Sixties as History: A Review of the Political Historiography,' *Reviews in American History* 33:1 (2–5), 133–152; and, Christopher B. Strain, *The Long Sixties: America, 1955–1973* (Hoboken, NJ: Wiley-Blackwell, 2016). For Reagan's conversion to conservatism, see, for instance: Thomas W. Evans, *The Education of Ronald Reagan: The General Electric Theatre Years* (New York: Columbia University Press, 2006).

17. *Desperate Journey*, directed by Raoul Walsh (Warner Bros, 1942).

18. *Roper Center*, 'How Groups Voted in 1984': https://ropercenter.cornell.edu/how-groups-voted-1984.

19. '1984 United States elections': https://profilbaru.com/article/1984_United_States_elections.

20. Heclo, 'The Mixed Legacies of Ronald Reagan,' 570–571.

21. Ambassador Wright despatch to Howe ("1984 US Presidential Election Result: What Will Reagan Do?"), 6 November 1984: https://www.margaretthatcher.org/document/233123.

22. Ambassador Wright despatch to Howe ("The 1984 US Presidential Election: Why Reagan Won"), 7 November 1984: https://www.margaretthatcher.org/document/233120.

23. Ibid.

24. See, for instance: M. J. Stephey, 'Top 10 Memorable Debate Moments,' *Time*: https://content.time.com/time/specials/packages/completelist/0,29569,1844704,00.html; Andrew Naughtie, 'Nine Presidential Debate Moments That Made American History,' *The Independent*, Thursday 24 September 2020: https://www.independent.co.uk/news/world/americas/us-election/presidential-debate-2020-history-reagan-clinton-trump-warren-b554073.html; and, Alex Browne, '8 of the Best Moments in Presidential Debates,' *History Hit*, 17 November 2021: https://www.historyhit.com/best-moments-in-presidential-debates/.

25. James Gerstenzang, 'Reagan Is Hailed as He Tells Bush to Win for Gipper,' *Los Angeles Times*, 16 August 1988: https://www.latimes.com/archives/la-xpm-1988-08-16-mn-683-story.html.

26. See: Al From, 'Recruiting Bill Clinton, How the New Democrats Recruited a Leader and Saved the Party AFTER Three Devastating Republican Routs,' *The Atlantic*, 3 December 2013: https://www.theatlantic.com/politics/archive/2013/12/recruiting-bill-clinton/281946/.

27. 'The Generation Gap and the 2012 Election,' *Pew Research Center*, 3 November 2011: https://www.pewresearch.org/politics/2011/11/03/the-generation-gap-and-the-2012-election-3/.
28. Dami Rosanwo and Madelyn Franz, 'The Next Generation and Music Discovery: Implications for Brands,' *The Harris Poll*, 28 October 2021: https://theharrispoll.com/briefs/music-and-branding/.
29. 'In Their Own Words: Obama on Reagan,' *The New York Times*: https://archive.nytimes.com/www.nytimes.com/ref/us/politics/21seelye-text.html?source=post_page--------------------------.
30. George W. Bush, 'Remarks by the President in Eulogy at National Funeral Service for Former President Ronald Wilson Reagan,' The National Cathedral, Washington, D.C., 11 June 2004: https://georgewbush-whitehouse.archives.gov/news/releases/2004/06/20040611-2.html.

SELECT BIBLIOGRAPHY

ARCHIVES AND KEY WEBSITES

Foreign Relations of the United States: https://history.state.gov/historicaldocuments.

Margaret Thatcher Foundation: https://www.margaretthatcher.org/.

Miller Center (University of Virginia): https://millercenter.org/.

National Security Archive: https://nsarchive.gwu.edu/.

Ronald Reagan Presidential Foundation and Institute: https://www.reaganfoundation.org/.

The American Presidency Project (University of California, Santa Barbara): https://www.presidency.ucsb.edu/.

DIARIES AND MEMOIRS

Brinkley, Douglas (ed.), Ronald Reagan, *The Reagan Diaries* (New York: HarperCollins, 2007).

Reagan, Ronald, *An American Life: The Autobiography* (New York, NY: Simon and Schuster, 1990).

Thatcher, Margaret, *The Downing Street Years* (London: Harper Collins, 1993).

© The Editor(s) (if applicable) and The Author(s), under exclusive
license to Springer Nature Switzerland AG 2024
J. Cooper et al., *Ronald Reagan's 1984*,
https://doi.org/10.1007/978-3-031-53677-9

INDEX

A
All of Me (film), 52, 84
Andropov, Yuri, 5, 26

B
Back to the Future (film), 85
Baker, James ('Jim'), 26, 32, 69, 71, 72
Beverly Hills Cop (film), 47–49, 53, 61
Brezhnev, Leonid, 5
Bush, George H.W., 6, 32, 97
Bush, George W., 8, 15, 16, 30, 32, 96, 97, 101

C
Carter, Jimmy, 4, 6–9, 12, 16, 29, 30, 59, 60, 64, 65, 68, 74, 95
Casey, William, 30
Central Intelligence Agency (CIA), 5, 15, 31, 68, 69
Chernenko, Konstantin, 5
China, 28, 37, 38

Clinton, Bill, 3, 6, 74, 94, 96, 97, 99
Conservative Party (U.K.), 24

D
D-Day commemorations, 39
Deaver, Michael, 21, 69, 73, 86, 89
Democratic National Convention (DNC), 97

F
Falklands War, 24
Ferraro, Geraldine, 59, 83
Footloose (movie), 44, 80

G
G7 Summit, 29, 39, 40
George Washington, George, 15
Ghostbusters (film), 3, 50, 52, 83
Go-Gos, The, 80
Goldbergs, The (television show), 92, 98
Gorbachev, Mikhail, 3, 5, 38, 94, 99

© The Editor(s) (if applicable) and The Author(s), under exclusive license to Springer Nature Switzerland AG 2024
J. Cooper et al., *Ronald Reagan's 1984*,
https://doi.org/10.1007/978-3-031-53677-9

106 INDEX

Grenada, 7, 10, 11, 32, 33
Greystoke (film), 53, 84

H
Hart, Gary, 38, 39, 57, 58, 97

I
Indiana Jones and the Temple of Doom (film), 52, 53, 85
Iran-Contra, 3, 6, 7, 13, 31, 32, 67, 68, 75

J
Joel, Billy, 44, 61, 79, 87

K
Karate Kid, The, 53
Khachigian, Ken, 61, 88
Kinnock, Neil, 26, 73

L
Lauper, Cyndi, 44, 80
Lincoln, Abraham, 1, 2, 6, 14, 30, 44
Loggins, Kenny, 44, 80

M
Madonna, 44, 80
McFarlane, Robert, 26, 32, 40, 69, 70, 72, 77, 78, 89
Mondale, Walter, 2, 23, 29, 38, 39, 57–60, 65–69, 83, 86–89, 92, 93, 97

N
Natural, The (film), 43, 48, 52, 82, 84
Nicaragua, 31, 32, 67–69

Nixon, Richard, 5, 6, 93

O
Obama, Barack, 1, 2, 12, 14, 96, 97
Olympics, 41, 42
Orwell, George, 2, 13, 44

P
Poindexter, John, 70

R
Reaganism, 3, 4, 8, 54, 93, 94, 98
Reagan, Nancy, 43
Reaganomics, 4, 8, 16, 41, 60, 87
Reagan Youth (punk band), 49
Red Dawn (film), 45, 53, 80, 81
Regan, Donald T., 25, 72
Republican National Convention (RNC), 43, 56, 57, 88
Rockwell, 44, 79
Roger and Me (film), 54
Romancing the Stone (film), 53, 84
Roosevelt, Franklin D., 1, 2, 29, 30, 44, 53, 58, 64, 88, 93
Run-D.M.C., 79, 82

S
Springsteen, Bruce, 44, 48–50, 79, 82, 83
State of the Union (speech), 26, 28, 76, 94
Strategic Defence Initiative (SDI or Star Wars), 9, 12, 25
Supertramp, 52, 80, 83
Swayze, Patrick, 45

T
Thatcher, Margaret, 9, 10, 17, 24, 40, 94, 95

INDEX 107

Trump, Donald, 3, 30, 93, 97
'Tuesday Team', 43
Turner, Tina, 44, 80

V

Vietnam (U.S. involvement in the war in Vietnam), 7, 28, 33, 53

W

Walters, Barbera, 65
Washington, George, 1, 2, 32, 44
Watergate, 3, 5, 7, 43
Wirthlin, Richard, 22, 23, 60, 71
Wright, Oliver, 94, 96, 97

Printed in the United States
by Baker & Taylor Publisher Services